Free to Learn

Introducing Steiner Waldorf Early Childhood Education

Lynne Oldfield

Preface by Dr. Cathy Nutbrown

School of Education, University of Sheffield

Foreword by Sally Jenkinson

Alliance for Childhood

Hawthorn Press

Published by Hawthorn Press, Hawthorn House, 1 Lansdown Lane, Stroud, Gloucestershire, GL5 1BJ, UK
Tel: (01453) 757040 Fax: (01453) 751138
hawthornpress@hawthornpress.com
www.hawthornpress.com

Illustrations by Rachel Oldfield.
Cover photo by Clare Benson (Lindens Kindergarten, Stroud, England)
Cover Design by Frances Fineran, Hawthorn Press.
Typesetting by Hawthorn Press, Stroud, Gloucestershire.
Printed in the UK by The Cromwell Press, Trowbridge, Wiltshire.

British Library Cataloguing in Publication Data applied for

ISBN 1 903 458 06 4

Photographs have been generously supplied by;

Clare Benson, Lao Kennish, Samantha Gowing (Lindens Kindergarten, Stroud, England)
Christina Korth (Michael Hall Kindergarten, Forest Row, England)
The Centre for Creative Education (Cape Town, South Africa)
Tina Bruinsma (Sloka Waldorf School, India)
Carol Cole (The Sophia Project, San Fransisco, USA)
Pat Hague (Eurythmist, London, England)
Erica Grantham (Emerson College, Forest Row, England)
The Taskia Nania Kindergarten (Penang, Malaysia)
The Panyotai Waldorf Kindergarten (Bangkok, Thailand)

Contents

Preface

'To everything there is a season'....time and purpose in early education

Dr. Cathy Nutbrown

To everything there is a season, and a time for every purpose....

Human life is lived in the context of changing times, changing seasons, changing perspectives. The Steiner Waldorf approach to education in the early years holds nature, the rhythm of the earth, cycles of life at its core. It is an approach to education where children play without the interference of adults, and as such the work of this particular movement in education can offer quite a different *'Foundation Stage'* from that introduced in England and Wales in 2000. (QCA 2000).

The Steiner Waldorf curriculum in early childhood education demonstrates many principles which would be endorsed by countless numbers of early childhood educators whether they work in the British state system, in Montessori nurseries, in voluntary Preschools and playgroups or in other non-mainstream early education settings. What does it mean to be *'Free to learn?'* The notion of things happening 'in their own time' is an important one to understand. When I chose the words from Ecclesiastes for the title of this preface I did so because, for me, they encapture the essence of patience in education. The importance of active patience, not passive waiting, but clear articulation of doing things *in their moment*. I have written elsewhere that the best way to get children ready for school at five is to let them be three when they are three and four when they are four (Nutbrown 1999). It is the hurry to create children who fit a policy-constructed view of childhood that leads to unrealistic pressure, not *just* on young children, but also on their parents and their teachers. So that is why it is important to re-iterate: '*To everything there is a season...*'

So, what are the common themes which all respectful educators of young children would want to ponder? In these pages, Lynne Oldfield repeatedly provides examples and explanations which suggest the importance of: respect for childhood; rhythm, repetition, security, continuity; and shared understandings.

Readers will find their own connections with these themes, but as a teacher and researcher whose work has been largely focused on the state system of early childhood education in the UK, I am prompted to reflect on these key issues.

Respect for childhood

Respecting childhood and children is an active undertaking, it is not *simply* a value position, it requires minute-by-minute action, giving children what they need when they need it and, importantly, giving them opportunities to 'be'. These are central to the demonstration of proper respect for childhood. Many of the examples in *Free to Learn* resonate with recent work on the care and education of children under three and provision for uninterrupted exploratory play. (Abbott and Moylett 1999). Respectful curricula which recognise children as capable learners depend upon responsible and articulate adults who know their role and why they respond to children as they do. Respect for childhood in early childhood education means having a clear rationale for practice; children need to play and learn alongside adults who know themselves.

Rhythm, repetition, security, continuity

Rhythm and repetition

The growing emphasis on *Emotional Intelligence*, what some now call '*Emotional Literacy*', advocates the importance of ample support and nourishment for children to become 'literate' in many ways – in their body, soul and mind. This is not about 'force feeding' of literacy skills too soon, but the provision of environments in which communication of ideas and emotions in a multiplicity of ways is valued and nurtured. Emotional literacy is about knowing one's self, and thereby finding ways to know others. In Steiner Waldorf kindergartens the security of *knowing* and *being* is grown through the rhythm of the day and the repetition of the familiar.

Rhythm and repetition form part of the experience of many adults throughout the world. For example, the holy rituals of many world religions provide structures for worship. Through faithful practices of meditation, recitation, prayer, penitence, fasting, celebration, and commemoration people connect with the spiritual. There is a security in these age-old practices, the security of faithful structures of devotion which become part of the life of many individuals.

Given the importance many adults attach to 'routine' we can understand the importance of these two constituents of daily life. For many adults the day begins with simple, yet important, personal routines of awakening (listening to a particular radio slot before getting up, putting on the kettle, letting the cat out, and so on). When such simple routines are disrupted (perhaps through the failure of the alarm clock) the rhythm of the whole day can be threatened! How much more important then, for children to know what will happen, when, and for the new challenges they experience through their play and interactions with others, to be massaged by the repetition of what is, for them, safe and familiar.

Security

Security, emotional security, can be born of the predictability of rhythm and repetition, but children also need protection from physical harm. In one weekend newspaper in early January 2001 I found four articles, each given at least half a page of broadsheet space, which demonstrated just how threatening our world can be: depleted uranium in Sarajevo where children played in a contaminated bomb crater; the abuse, torture and murder of an eight-year-old girl in a London flat where she lived; controversy in the UK over the measles, mumps and rubella (MMR) vaccine alleged to cause or contribute to autism in some children; the kidnapping of a six-year-old child in the Philippines. Such articles appear on the television news and in our newspapers with such regularity that we sometimes become numbed to their horror. The threats to safety can be rolled off the tongue with alarming familiarity: BSE, GM foods, mobile phones, immunisation, traffic pollution, pollution of the seas and rivers…the list could go on.

The need to protect children is not new, but the threats to their well-being have changed over the past century. Robert Owen's first school for infants in New Lanark provided a haven for young children of factory workers in the early 1800s, catering for their physical and intellectual needs, and ensuring some space to play, (Owen 1824). In the 1920s the MacMillan sisters promoted good health as well as learning in their 'Open Air' nurseries. Fresh air, hot food and cleanliness became the priorities for children from the slum areas of the cities in the British Isles because many children suffered from rickets and malnutrition as effects of poverty (Aldrich and Gordon 1989).

Arguably, it was Susan Isaacs who moved on thinking about the education of the young to include their immense capacity to imitate and imagine in their play. Isaacs left an enduring legacy of understanding children's play in the detailed observations of children who attended her Malting House School 1924-1927, (Isaacs 1954).

Providing for children's play, and the threats to such play, was debated throughout the 20th Century. In the 70s Niko Tinbergen (1976) wrote an article called *The importance of being playful* in which he identified the difference for children whose parents once played outdoors, unsupervised, making mud pies, free to explore. He warned that nurseries were forced to create the 'muddy field' in a small tray of clay, and puddles and rivers were experiences through 'water trough'. So what happens when those children become parents, how do parents who have never experienced the importance of being playful understand and create the opportunities for their children to know what playing – *really playing* is? These are important questions for all early childhood educators, the question of setting children free to play and at the same time protecting them and ensuring the physical care they must have.

Continuity

Home and school (whatever form that might take) are two key places in most children's lives. The importance of continuity of experience between these two is crucial for young children. They need continuity not just within these two settings but also *between* them. That is why communication between teachers and parents is vital for the emotional and intellectual health of children. This is born out of respect and information. Educators have a duty to share their philosophy and practices with parents, just as parents have a responsibility to their children to share with school, the needs, anxieties and excitements of their children; (that does not mean that parents 'tell tales ' on their children, but that there is some attempt to keep all adults informed about the child's 'state'). By such means, the security of children can be generated and sustained, and learning can be 'continuous' with everyday life.

Shared understandings

There is a rich variety of approaches to early childhood education in the UK and around the world. What is important is not so much the identification of the *best* single approach, but the reaching of shared understandings of various approaches and thus the shared *principles* from which the pursuit of practices which are *good for children* can emanate. For example, Reggio Emilia, in Northern Italy, has become internationally renowned for its approach to early childhood education. It is constructed on the principles of children's rights and children's multiple ways of communicating and exploring – referred to often as *The Hundred Languages*. Much has been written about this approach (see for example Abbott and Nutbrown 2000), but this is not to say that Reggio Emilia is *the* approach. It would be folly, the ultimate in disrespect for childhood, to insist that all early childhood education in every country in the world adopted this approach. As Martin Woodhead (1996) ably demonstrates, quality is culturally defined and identified. It is not the transportation and importation of ideas and practices which are important, but the shared understanding of many approaches.

Early childhood educators, whatever their setting, should understand something of the underpinning principles, central practices and guiding philosophies of a range of approaches to early childhood education. It is by this means that we are able to make choices, choices about our own work and practices, and choices for our children in their early years. Sharing understandings does not mean adopting the practices of others wholesale, for example my own work on early literacy development would not 'fit' with the Steiner philosophy for kindergarten years, but that does not stop me from learning about Steiner ways of thinking and doing, and it does not prevent those early educators working in the Steiner movement learning about the things which are important to other early childhood educators. Shared understanding does not invite the 'cloning' of early years education practices, rather it invites the healthiest form of informed diversity. Many shared understandings can also identify shared roots, with the connecting work of

Montessori, Froebel, Isaacs, all of which advocated, in their different ways, the importance of play, the importance of watching and of *active patience*.

Constructions of childhoods

'I'd like to go to a school where there was a beautiful garden, and trees, and woods, and flowers, and in the middle of the garden there would be a cool pool, a big pool where the dolphins swim... '

Six-year-old Martha had her own clear idea of what a perfect school should be like. It should be a place where the beauty of nature was right there at the heart of everything that happened. *In the middle* would be calm, and grace and beauty. Had Martha met the HMI Christian Schiller they might well have had an interesting conversation about what schools should be like, and what children should do in them. In 1946 when Schiller gave his characteristics of a 'good' school, he wrote that:

- the school conceives of primary education, not as a preparation for something to follow, but as a fulfilment of a stage of development;
- the school seeks to achieve this fulfilment, not by securing certain standards of attainment, but by providing in abundance such experience and activities as will enable all the children to develop to the full at each phase of growth;
- the children are expressing their powers in language, in movement, in music, in painting, and in making things – that is to say, as artists;
- the children are developing their powers in language, in observation, in counting, and in the use of the body – that is to say, as workmen;
- the children are learning to live together to the best advantage;

- the children's need for movement and for rest determine the arrangement of experience and activities, and how much the children get out of an experience or activity determines the amount of time given to it;
  (Schiller 1946 in Griffin-Bale(ed) 1979 p.3)

I have chosen six of Schillers' many characteristics of a 'good' school. But it is clear that, for this member of Her Majesty's Inspectorate, the values which underpinned education were the needs and capabilities of children *as perceived by an adult.* Thus was constructed a view of childhood as a time of active engagement, of exploration and a time too where adults must provide some protection.

In the early 21st century most children must live their childhoods according to adult definitions of what childhood is. Steiner education, with its own construction of childhood, seeks to create living and learning experiences in the early years which foster the development of the *Will.* Within this philosophy all other things, curriculum, attitude, organisation, practice, responsibilities, flow to create a holistic experience for young children. Central is the need to nurture children; to nurture the emotional *and* the cognitive; the body, mind *and* the soul; and in so doing to create a form of early education which both challenges and protects children and their childhoods.

Legacies of freedom
In 1983, Carl Rogers' famous book *Freedom to Learn* was republished for the 80's. In the introduction Rogers wrote:

Our educational system is, I believe, failing to meet the real needs of our society. I have said that our schools, generally, constitute the most traditional, conservative, rigid, bureaucratic institution of our time, and the institution most resistant to change. I stand by that statement, but it does not describe the whole situation. There are new

developments – alternative schools, open classrooms, opportunities for
independent study- all kinds of adventurous enterprises being carried
on by dedicated teachers and parents. One of my purposes in bringing
out this book is to encourage these new trends, these new hopes in the
educational world, and to point the way to still further advances.
(Rogers 1983 p.1)

Of course, Steiner education can hardly be described as a 'new trend'; it is well rooted in the history of education of the 20th Century, but when traditions and practices are shared, Steiner approaches will represent for some, a *new* discovery. It will represent, for some, a revelation that this established approach to education could offer a grounded and articulated alternative to other established approaches. Carl Rogers' book opens with the words of Albert Einstein who said:

It is a fact nothing short of a miracle that the modern methods of
instruction have not yet entirely strangled the holy curiosity of inquiry;
for this delicate little plant, aside from stimulation, stands mainly in
need of freedom; without this it goes to wrack and ruin without fail.

Throughout the legacies of history, international conflicts, and the undaunted work of yesterday's and today's pioneers, those with a commitment to providing the best they can for children in their earliest years have debated the ingredients of curriculum and the responsibilities of educators. If we have learned anything from our history in early childhood education then surely we have learned that work with children in early childhood settings – Steiner, Montessori, Preschool Playgroups, state nurseries, reception classes, independent schools, wherever the education of the young takes place – surely we have learned that successful education of young children depends upon the development of a *healthy culture of relationships*. Those relationships depend upon learning with and from others, others in our own learning community, and beyond to wider local, national and international possibilities. The dissemination of information and the potential for human contact and communication (albeit sometimes 'virtually') means that it is possible for early childhood educators all over the world to exchange news and information with their colleagues. There is no excuse now at the birth of the third modern millennium for ignorance of the work of others. With greater sharing we inherit the legacies of freedom, freedom to act together, freedom to learn, freedom to understand and the freedom to be different.

'To everything there is a season ....'

Dr Cathy Nutbrown
lectures and researches at the School of Education,
University of Sheffield

References from Preface

Abbott, L. and Moylett, H. (1999) *Working with the Under threes: supporting children's needs* Buckingham: OUP

Aldrich, R. and Gordon, P. (1989) *Dictionary of British Educationists* London: Woburn Press

Isaacs, S, (1954) *The Educational Value of the Nursery School* London: British Association of Early Childhood Education

Nutbrown, C. (1999) *Threads of Thinking: Young children learning and the role of early education* London Paul Chapman Publishing

Nutbrown, C. (ed) (1997) *Respectful Educators – Capable Learners: Children's Rights and Early Education* London: Paul Chapman Publishing

Owen, R (1824) An outline of the system at New Lanark (Glasgow 1824) pp 32-33 – Select Committee on Education of the Lower Orders of the Metropolis (London 1816: 1968 edition)

In a shelter for homeless families children find pleasure and comfort in making their own 'house'
The Sophia Project, San Francisco USA

QCA (2000) The Foundation Stage London: Qualifications and Curriculum Authority

Schiller, C (1979) *Christian Schiller in his own words.* Edited by C. Griffiths-Blake London: National Association for Primary Education

Tinbergen, N. (1976) *The importance of being playful* London: British Association of Early Childhood Education

Woodhead, M. (1996) *In search of the rainbow* Netherlands: The Van Leer Foundation

Free to Learn

Foreword

Respecting Childhood

For almost 80 years in as many different contexts and cultures, from the Favelas in Sao Paulo to the townships in South Africa, Steiner Waldorf education has provided early childhood care and education for some of the world's children. Described as 'this most modest movement', its kindergartens and schools have consistently striven to give children the highest quality of educational nurturing in their early years. Different kindergartens vary according to local needs, but what remains constant is a deeply held belief that childhood matters; that the early years are not a phase of life to be rushed through, but constitute a stage of tremendous importance needing to be experienced fully in its own right.

Underpinning this book is the conviction that the child's early learning is profound; that quality of early experience is every bit as important as quantity. It is a book which implicitly acknowledges that the way we learn, as well as what we learn, will set the arrow of our future on its particular course, for better or for worse.

It has always been difficult to be a child. The risks involved in getting through childhood unharmed were, and still are, tremendous. Too many children still face poverty, neglect, disease, abandonment and prejudice. Every age and every community is fraught with its own particular set of challenges for its youngest members, and our age is no exception. Whilst apparently benefiting from a better standard of living (a full tummy does not automatically signal a good diet), the reality is that our children are subject to a whole range of new and insidious pressures specific to our times. In our speeded-up world, growing numbers of young children are registering feelings of stress and disorientation. They experience life as going too fast for them. They feel unable to 'keep up', and they live in fear of failure. Our highly competitive society does little to relieve their anxieties despite evidence that disengaged, frustrated and unhappy children are far more likely to become disaffected adolescents.

In the United Kingdom, testing begins at four. Is it any wonder that feelings of insecurity and panic are endemic? Education seems to have become a process of diminishing returns - impoverishing the child. David Elkind, the psychologist and social commentator, suggests that rather than vertical acceleration, children need 'horizontal enrichment'. This book demonstrates one form of horizontal enrichment in practice.

Further pressures affecting our children include the phenomenal over-exposure to the synthetic world of the television, computer and video, coupled with an under-exposure to the natural environment. Where are the places for children to play today? Where can they make their own discoveries, forge friendships, create their own worlds and become active participants rather than passive, alienated consumers? Drugs are increasingly used to control children's disruptive behaviour, and one cannot help but wonder whether children are becoming disruptive because their natural exuberance and need to be active has no outlet? Television, 'the plug-in drug', and other forms of technological entertainment militate against creativity and the expending of healthy childhood energy. Though technology keeps children quiet and gives over-worked parents a bit of peace, at core it fails to satisfy. Superficially engaging, at deeper levels the active child, stilled by the electronic babysitter, experiences dissatisfaction and disappointment. The Waldorf educational curriculum consciously incorporates many of the things children formerly experienced after school in their 'spare time' (a concept inimical to many today) in 'TV-free' urban and rural play environments. Both learning and play are being taken out of children's hands, literally and metaphorically; and they are losing autonomy on all fronts.

With quiet authority, this book outlines a reassuring picture of healthy stress-free childhood. It reminds us of the importance of rhythm and security, of the need for sensory encounters and the centrality of play in early childhood. The Waldorf model is founded on the premise that living fully in the present is the best preparation for the future.

A counterpoint to pressurized, synthetic childhood, the thoughts and ideas presented here align with the aims and objectives of *The Alliance for Childhood*, a forum for groups, organizations and individuals working together out of respect for childhood in a world-wide effort to improve children's lives (see Appendix 3). The Alliance recognizes the need for educators to address children's issues in new and creative ways. Based as it is on a tried and tested educational system, this book offers some up-to-date solutions for current problems affecting children across the social spectrum. It offers new and exciting ways of seeing children and their educational experience. It recognizes and addresses the critical roles of the parent and the teacher, and above all it values and respects the child. It is a book for our times.

Sally Jenkinson
*Works for the Alliance for Childhood, formerly Early Years
Consultant, Steiner Waldorf Schools Fellowship of Great Britain and
kindergarten teacher. Author of* **The Genius of Play**

Time for dreamy reflection *Kindergarten, South Africa*

Time and Space for Children - Introducing Free to Learn

Lynne Oldfield

At the beginning of this new millennium so much is being expected of our young children. The burden of expectation arrives in many forms – early formal learning and assessment; the break-up of the family unit; hectic schedules of baby-gym, ballet and language classes as 'quality time' replaces play time; away-from-home care even before a child's first birthday…

On the one hand our children are constantly being 'hyped up' with a 'fast track' culture and a technological bombardment from computers, videos and television; whilst at the same time an increasing number of children are being 'hyped down' with behaviour modifying drugs such as Ritalin. Too much too soon, and little of what is really needed – the time and space to be a child. The time given to childhood is constantly eroded as children are hurried toward the adult world. The disappearance of childhood is a contemporary phenomenon arising from a disappearing understanding of the true needs of early childhood.

In 1762 the Swiss writer Jean Rousseau published *Emile*. He was attempting to define the impact of education upon the young developing child, and the need for 'educators' – both parents and teachers – to be willingly responsible for this impact. Most significantly he introduced a new concept, the right of the child to have childhood acknowledged as a time of unique developmental laws and qualities.

In 1840 the German educationalist Friedrich Froebel (1782-1852) used the beautifully descriptive word 'kinder-garten' to describe an educational environment in which this right would be respected – truly a Child's Garden. For Froebel, the teacher's task was to help the child overcome any obstacles to the healthy unfolding of his own unique destiny. He was acutely aware of the role of environmental influences in determining the full realization of the child's potential and his respect for children's play was profound. 'Playing is the self-education of the child.'

In the last century childhood was again honoured through the work of the two giants of early childhood education, the Italian Maria Montessori (1870-1952) and the Austrian Rudolf Steiner (1861-1925), who was the founder of Waldorf education. Both presented educational insights which were to be taken up worldwide, and which have endured because the methods used are only secondary to the principles and ideals which inspire their practice. What mattered most was that a curriculum for the early years of childhood should be meaningful; that the practitioner was clear as to *why* she was creating the particular educational environment. The answer always rested upon an understanding of the child's development.

Froebel, Montessori and Steiner accentuated the active, do-ing nature of the young child, and explored the possible paths toward self-identity and self-discipline through the child's self-initiated, independent activity. Their interpretation and understanding of how this activity should be supported differed, but they shared a respect for the child's active nature. They also held the spirituality of the child in the highest regard, and for Rudolf Steiner in particular this was always meant to be the starting point for the teacher's relationship to the children in his care.

This book is an attempt to introduce the 'will-first' pedagogy of Steiner Waldorf early childhood education. Waldorf daycare, parent and child, and kindergarten settings are centres where a 'be active' rather than 'sit still' culture prevails, with the much desired qualities of attentiveness and self-control emerging from the active experience.

The chapters which follow will first present Rudolf Steiner's view of humanity, which is the prime source of inspiration for Waldorf education. The will (active) aspect of child development in the first seven years is then presented with examples of how Waldorf early childhood teachers specifically work with this in a positive way. Other principles are then introduced – for example, how the use of imitation, rhythm and a conscious use of sensory nourishment guide this will-nature towards self-control and the habit of self-direction, laying a firm foundation for school readiness. Later chapters reveal the extent and range of initiatives arising from the inspiration of Waldorf education.

The educational principles presented are not all unique to Waldorf education and early childhood educators working with young children, in the many and varied settings, will find much that is common ground. It is not so much the differences between the various approaches to early years education which are of interest but the shared insight which brings confirmation of the way forward into the future.

The first Waldorf kindergarten opened in Stuttgart, Germany, in 1926, one year after the death of Rudolf Steiner. In the past decade there has been an obvious acceleration of interest in this form of education. Around the world Waldorf initiatives are constantly beginning. After 25 years as a Waldorf kindergarten teacher, my own enthusiasm for this work is ever rekindled as I experience the continuing relevance of Waldorf's fundamental principles for the healthy development of children.

The child's imitation of her surroundings now has added meaning in the light of the negative images to which so many children are exposed and which have such a drastic effect upon their behaviour. The value of a steady, rhythmical, reassuring existence gains significance when we observe the effect of erratic and exhausting lifestyles upon children's health and general well-being. Recent research into the effect of over-stimulation upon the brain's development alerts us to the need for a discriminating attitude toward sensory experience in the early years of childhood. The growing concern about hyperactivity highlights the urgent need for a fundamental review of our attitude toward the movement needs of young children.

My own work as an experienced Waldorf early childhood teacher increasingly reveals an education which, far from being anachronistic, appears ever more radically 'ahead of its time' in what it has to offer parents and teachers as a guiding star in their earnest and loving efforts to be with children in an understanding and confident way. I value enormously the inspiring presence of a true idealism in what I do, and the freedom to bring this idealism into practical expression each day in my kindergarten.

It is my hope that the contents of this book will, in some way, inspire all those who find themselves in the company of a young child to be courageous in their own efforts to protect the child's right to a healthy childhood.

Lynne Oldfield
February 2001

'Faced with the stark reality that childhood is fast disappearing, Lynne Oldfield quietly convinces us that there is still hope: the richness and quality of the Waldorf Early Childhood experience she evokes recreates and protects the lost world of childhood, but the benefits spill over, touching the lives of parents, educators and community alike. Vividly and sensitively written, this book has a powerful message for anyone concerned with the state of childhood today.'
Dr Helen Prochazka, Chairman Montessori Education UK

About the Author and Illustrator

Lynne Oldfield, BA (Hons), Dip. Waldorf Early Childhood Education, has worked for twenty four years as a Waldorf Kindergarten teacher and twelve years as a Director of the London Waldorf Early Childhood Teacher Training Course. She has written extensively for various Waldorf publications and is a lecturer on themes of parenting, Waldorf education and early childhood development. She also works at the Linden Kindergarten in Stroud, Gloucestershire.

Rachel Oldfield, BA (Hons) Illustration, attended Wynstones Waldorf School in Gloucestershire, England from the age of three to eighteen. After graduating from Brighton University she did volunteer work as a muralist in a school in Southern India before returning to England to work with murals, mosaics and Illustration. She is currently illustrating her second book.

This book is dedicated to my family – Lichen, Maya, Rachel, Manny, Sophia and David.

It has been written with the ever present memory of Caragh Joy, Jacob and Elsa-Luna, who graced my kindergarten with their presence.

It would not have been completed without the support and contributions of many people – series editor Richard House; publisher Martin Large; translator Pauline Wehrle; my colleague Sally Jenkinson; and the contributors who took the time from their own demanding and valuable work with children to respond to my request for information. Thank you.

Free to Learn…
The Lindens Kindergarten, Stroud, England.

PART I

THE WALDORF KINDERGARTEN EXPERIENCE

Smell, touch, sight, sound – the senses are nourished!
The Lindens Kindergarten, Stroud, England.

Chapter 1

Experiencing the Waldorf Kindergarten: Children, Parents, Teachers

In a Waldorf kindergarten it is the actual experience and the qualities which emerge in the children as a result of the experience which are central – and which probably constitute the main basis upon which parents choose a Waldorf kindergarten for their child. In this chapter, a series of personal experiences of kindergartens are presented from the points of view of the various parties involved – children, parents and teachers.

From the Children's Point of View

Time to breathe out

With the first step across the threshold of a Waldorf kindergarten room, children enter an environment which positively invites them to become active. They are immediately confronted with images of 'doing' – teachers and children are expressing their 'love of action'.

The teacher works at the heart of all the activity, a calm, steady focal point within an atmosphere of enthusiasm and purpose, generated by her work and the children's play. She is already busy with the day's regular activity, perhaps preparing dough for bread-making – sifting, pouring, kneading, shaping. Inevitably she is joined by a group of children who have come of their own free will, drawn toward her by their natural impulse to imitate. They are readily included, for the teacher is always well prepared in advance for this natural response, with extra bowls, spoons and child-sized aprons at hand. No instructions are given, but the teacher's clear and logical movements will convey what needs to be done. Later the smell of freshly baked bread fills the room.

An assistant teacher is preparing the morning's snack at another table. Three of the six year olds come to help. They wash their hands and then fetch small chopping boards, knives and a bowl. After two years in the group they have come to expect the freedom to take initiative in this way; and the well-ordered environment, with everything in its proper place and accessible, makes this impulse possible. Apples are peeled and chopped, oranges squeezed, the mixture stirred. Then a logical progression of activity follows – the bowl of muesli will be covered with a freshly laundered muslin cloth; utensils will be taken to the kitchen sink, washed and dried and put back in their regular place. The scraps will be taken to the compost. Some children choose to help scrub the table and then shine it with beeswax polish. Now the table must be set. Place-mats, bowls, spoons, mugs, a vase of flowers and a candle on a cloth of coloured silk. A chair must be found for each setting. The children join in with confidence, for they know the routine well. This is the way it is done every day.

Nothing is rushed. The children sense that there is plenty of time to do things well.
Nothing to fear. Each child has come to trust the certainty of the morning's rhythm.
Nothing to fail. In place of failure is the satisfaction which children experience when they are allowed to play.
No instructions. Instead, self-direction and the willingness to imitate.

The room has a reassuring, homelike, atmosphere which is immediately familiar to a young child and strengthens his trust in the new experience. Around the teacher's mood of domestic purpose the rest of the room 'hums' with spontaneous creativity. The group will normally consist of a 'family' of mixed-age children from three to six years of age, a comforting experience in a time of the fragmentation of the traditional family unit. The children will usually remain with the same teacher for three years, bringing elements of consistency and continuity which are so valuable for this age group. The teacher will come to know them and their families well and so be able to guide their development. Single children, particularly those in single-parent families, benefit from these family-like groupings. The three years olds look up to the six year olds; and the six year olds develop a responsible, caring gesture toward the younger ones.

Each child will express himself in the characteristic way of his age group, yet with the stamp of his own individuality. Most of the three year olds can be found close by the comforting presence of a teacher, or else dreamily observing – and learning from – the activities of the older children. Four to five year olds quite typically enter the space and walk purposefully toward the play equipment, perhaps a collection of boxes and planks in a far corner. Boxes are then set end-to-end and bound together with pieces of ropes; planks placed on top, a chair on top of the planks. The train's driver gets into position and calls his passengers to 'come on board'. The London-bound train has departed!

With teacher's help, a four year old turns a table upside down, attaches an upended broom to one leg and ties a tea towel to the end of the broom. Coloured clothes are tacked around the four sides. He then lifts a chair into the centre and takes up his position. He's 'gone fishing' but says he will be back in time for snack.

Two six-year-old girls have pulled a small table into one corner of the room and covered it with a green silk scarf. They go to a nearby cupboard and take out a basket of puppet figures. The figures are then placed in a landscape which has been built up with shells, pieces of driftwood and coloured fleece. A puppet show then begins: 'Anyone want to come and see our puppet show?'. Chairs are dragged over and arranged... Not enough! - they need two more. The problem is solved and then a teacher is invited to tell the story.

A group of six-year-old boys and girls is sitting at a table weaving on small handlooms. There is a steady flow of conversation as they work and they maintain their efforts for a considerable length of time and over a number of days. Meanwhile, the 'train' has been abandoned as the driver and his passenger have moved off to join the assistant, who is busy sanding down pieces of wood which will be made into candle-stick holders for the Christmas Fair. The 'driver' is now a 'carpenter' and some four year olds have taken up the boxes and made bunk-beds for the dolls.

The room will have been well prepared for this glorious activity. Baskets of wood, pebbles, coloured cloths of silk and cotton, ribbons and rope, wooden planks, smoothed and oiled by the children, boxes, stands – raw materials are provided to serve the children's endless imaginings.

Time to breathe in

For an hour children will be allowed to move freely within this atmosphere of artistic activity, play and domestic work. Then the teachers commence to restore order in their working space; cloths are carefully folded, chairs returned to the table, tools put away. Dolls are put to sleep and boats are led back to the harbour. All the children come to recognize these signals. It is 'clearing up' time. The teacher might begin to sing a song which she always sings at this transition moment in the morning.

> *I met a little dusty gnome.*
> *He said it's time to clean my home:*
> *Round, round, round;*
> *Swish, swish, swish -*
> *Clean my home.*

Some of the older children sing with her, but all of the children join in the activity of putting everything back in its rightful place, in readiness for the next day. The room is abuzz with busy-ness. Then slowly the room is cleared and the children settle. The open, child-directed time of free play will now be balanced by a teacher-led ring-time. The children gather in a circle and begin to imitate the teacher's words and gestures as she leads them through an imaginative experience with the use of verse, song and action. First, a morning verse:

I stand as tall as an old oak tree,
I stretch out to the stars.
I want to enfold the world.
We are family.
Good morning. Good morning.

Then off they go, following their teacher. The season will determine the choice of theme. Autumn might see them shaking apples from the trees, becoming scampering, nut-collecting squirrels or woodchoppers 'tall and strong'. No pressure to perform, no pressure to memorize the words (but as stories and ring-times are repeated over a number of days, the children soon learn the words effortlessly through repetition). They feel the pleasure and security of being caught up in the imagination and the ease of being led by the teacher's example – all within the comfort of a shared, communal experience.

Gathered together in such a natural way, they are now ready for snack-time, which they have helped to prepare – and ready to sit at the table which they helped to set. But first, a visit to the washroom and the washing of hands in warm, lavender-scented water. The bustle of returning to the room and finding a place to sit is soon settled by the teacher with a verse and the lighting of a candle.

For the golden corn, and the apples on the tree;
For the golden butter, and the honey for my tea.
For fruits and nuts and flowers, that grow along the way;
For birds and beasts and flowers, we give thanks every day.

The older children serve the food and pour the drinks, and soon a comfortable family-like mood surrounds the scene. Conversations begin between children and teachers, child and friend. The end of this happy time is signalled when one of the children takes her turn to extinguish the candle with a snuffer; plates and mugs are placed in baskets, ready for washing, and chairs are carried to the centre of the room in preparation for story-time at the end of the morning.

So many natural opportunities present themselves for the children to take initiative, be active in meaningful ways, to practise language skills and develop attentiveness, to learn valuable social skills and life skills that make sense to them because they arise from the context of daily life. The entire mood is natural, unforced. Each day, in this non-stressful way, they develop increasing confidence and self-control. They are being shown, with understanding and patience, how to take their place within the human community.

Later, when this important foundation stage in their education is completed, other teachers can direct their attention to the world of numeracy and literacy. But first things first!

Time to breathe out
Now to become freely active once again and to practise self-direction. The children ready themselves for outdoor play – hats, gloves, coats, wellingtons – more opportunity to take initiative, to self-help and to help others. The family mood continues as the

older children help the little ones with their clothing and the little ones attempt to imitate the independence of the six year olds.

Creative play will now develop in the outdoor space which will have been designed, wherever possible, to encourage imaginative play and to enable the children to be surrounded with rich, sensory experience. The teachers will continue to be 'enthusiastic workers' and the children are free to join them in their work or to initiate their own independent play.

In autumn, leaves will be swept and added to the compost heap. The vegetable garden is dug over. Apples are gathered and a hand-operated apple press might be used to produce fresh apple juice and pulp for jam-making. The Harvest Festival will include bulb planting in the 'lap of Mother Earth'. (The teachers use rich, pictorial language whenever appropriate, nourishing imagination and creative expression. The quality of language is considered to be of importance.) As Winter closes in, strings of peanuts are put out for the birds, and garden tools are washed, oiled and stored away. The springtime offers the excitement of finding the first snowdrop. Vegetables are planted in the prepared soil; fleece washed and dyed, spun by the teacher and woven by the older children. At the Easter festival, egg hunts lead to the discovery of eggs in mossy nests made by the children. Summer allows the washing of clothes which are hung out to dry in the sun, then gathered into the washing basket, folded and ironed. Plants are watered and herbs brought in for drying in time for winter, to be used later in the making of soup for snack-time.

The seasons offer their own unique curriculum, yielding a vast supply of learning opportunities rooted in practical activities. (Of course these activities will vary from country to country.) The children develop a relationship to time as each season returns and reveals its rhythmical activities. Superimposed upon this rolling, cyclical landscape of the seasons, the festivals stand as beacons, offering points of heightened activity. Work and play interweave, and the natural enthusiasm of childhood is welcomed and allowed expression. Childhood is honoured, respected and given time.

Indoors, the baskets of raw materials have inspired play; outdoors, Nature provides all the necessary experience and materials for joyful, creative activity. And a sensory feast!... smell, sight, sound, touch. A physical celebration!... mud pies, constructing a den, building a dam, making a sandcastle. The joy of discovery!... snails, ladybirds, spiders' webs. Balancing a plank over a log to make a see-saw, language skills developed in conversations with friends, social interaction with its own 'learning curve'. A peaceful, dreamy, private moment hiding beneath a bush.

An hour quickly passes as limbs are stretched, physical skills tested, social connections strengthened. The teachers begin to put away tools, bring in the wheelbarrows and watering cans. The children recognize another signal. It is 'clearing up' time again. Wellies off (and side by side!); coats on pegs, slippers back on (older children can help the little ones). Wash hands. (Good habits – the foundation for later self-discipline – have been established through imitation and reinforced with repetition.)

Time to breathe in

Story time. Chairs have been placed in a half-circle – this is the 'moon boat' which will sail away to the 'land of fairy-tale'. The children settle into quiet attentiveness after the energetic bustle of outdoor play. The teacher places a candle-lit lantern beside his chair. Little hands come together to make a 'boat' as the 'story song' is sung:

Mother of the fairy-tale,
Take me by your silver hand;
Sail me in your silver boat,
Sail me silently afloat.
Mother of the fairy-tale,
Take me to your shining land.

And then it begins, with those magical words, 'Once upon a time, many years ago....'. (The traditional fairy-tales and stories, linked to the seasons, provide a rich language experience to nourish the inner life of the child. During story-time the child is still 'active' but now inwardly, as she re-creates the pictures unfolding through the story.)

As the last words are spoken, the story-teller leaves a brief moment for utter silence - the sound of silence - as the little listeners absorb the richness of the tale. The candle is 'put to rest'. It is time to go home.

Goodbye now, goodbye now – it's time to go, or we'll be late.
Goodbye now, goodbye now – goodbye to all of you.
It's time to go, or we'll be late;
Let's all go outside, to the gate –
Goodbye now, goodbye now – goodbye to all of you.

Parental Points of View

Julia and Mike Willoughby, Orana Waldorf School, Canberra, Australia, write:

'As parents we see education as far more than learning academic skills. It needs to involve the development of the whole child – emotionally, physically, intellectually and spiritually. We feel that Steiner schools address all these areas in a loving and caring way.

To survive in an ever-changing world, children need to feel whole inside, confident in their abilities to do the best they can and be able to interact well socially. We also feel that the world is very stressful, both for the adult and the child, and children need to have a simple, undamaged childhood in order to develop a sense of inner strength. The Steiner school gives them this, and when I see my five year old drift out of the kindergarten, at the end of the day, contented and at peace, I know that she has been in the right place.

We also admire the dedication and self-awareness of the teaching staff. They also have this sense of peacefulness, and treat the children with such respect. They make wonderful role models for both the children and for us, the parents.

Finally, Waldorf education offers a wonderful community for the whole family. Whilst all parents may not have the same views of philosophy on life, we mostly share a desire for our children to develop into sensitive, caring individuals who can make a difference in this often troubled world.'

Sue Charman, Rosebridge Steiner Kindergarten, Cambridge, England, writes:

'When I first sat in a Steiner kindergarten I felt that I had come home. Here my children would be free to develop the skills of a natural enquirer after knowledge. They would not be forced, however kindly, to perform feats of early intellectual achievement which would leave them uninspired, without curiosity, at an early age. Nor would this education require of them to fail and fail again to grasp concepts that, no matter how convincingly they parrot them, remain beyond their reach.

Here they would develop in a natural rhythm. They would find adults turning wheat into bread, wood into tools, cloth into puppets. They would be in a mixed age group which would require them to take care of the younger ones, and for the little ones to look up to, and learn from, the older children. Life would be about imagination and wonder, nature and community – but would not yet be about maths and writing.

As a parent I have enjoyed enormously my involvement in the festivals, parent evenings, social events. The children seem to have a great self-esteem and self-confidence as well as creativity and curiosity. These are great tools for the future, worth so much more than being able to read and write at an early age. In a few years they will be able to do these things; but will the children who have learned to read and write so early have made up for their lost play-time, or will they have settled in for a life of being "taught" rather than seeking to learn?'

Sudha and Ravi Madhuri, Sloka Waldorf School, India, write:

'In India, most parents send their children to school when the child is just two-and-a-half. Reading, writing and numeracy are taught from that early age in mainstream education. Given the premium on education in India, choosing a school for your child is a very important decision. If we were to paint the picture of our dream school, it would be a place where a child is enabled in the process of learning. It would be a place which is both peaceful and at one with nature. There would be joy in discovery and in the spirit of enquiry. There would be sharing and giving and the development of community. A place shaped by everyone who loves children and childhood.

The Waldorf School, Sloka, promised to come close to that ideal and, in retrospect, has not disappointed us. The focus on the complete child is meaningfully developed, and emotional well-being and the kindling of the human spirit are taken up with dedication by the teachers. This education appears to allow children to be children and to grow at a natural pace.'

Supita Warunpitikul, Panyotai Waldorf Kindergarten, Bangkok, Thailand, writes:

'Whilst other kindergartens focus mainly on intellectual development, Panyotai Waldorf kindergarten attends to the development of the will and spiritual nature of the child. In the process, children see the value of creating for themselves – which is very important in our age when consumerism is widespread, even in education. In such a world, children only learn to accept ready answers rather than to ask questions and seek the answers for themselves. Nowadays the line between right and wrong has become blurred, so how can they make decisions about the problems they encounter in life?

As childhood has become more fragile from the effects of the social environment, inner strength is important. Rather than perceiving the world only in the sensible and rational aspects, here the children are in touch with trust and reverence, which I think is more important than information and knowledge. Even though in the future they will meet with more difficult and complicated situations, they will still have the forces to change it for the better.'

Kimiko Miyashita, Taska Nania Waldorf Kindergarten, Penang, Malaysia, writes:

'I am a Japanese mother of two daughters. When I sent my eldest daughter to a kindergarten in Japan I was only interested in early intellectual development for her. When we moved to Malaysia due to my husband's work I placed Naho, my second daughter, in Taska Nania, the Waldorf school, where many other Japanese children go and the teacher is Japanese. Nine months later I moved her to an International School for a more intellectual approach. During the two weeks trial at the new school she was never happy and longed to return to Taska Nania, so eventually I allowed her to return. She was a shy and quiet child and now she is much more active and enthusiastic. Naho's development at the kindergarten struck me as being well balanced and guided in a natural way. There is no undue stress or emotional trauma, and she gets to enjoy her childhood amongst peers, develop social skills and discover herself, as well as developing self-direction in the learning process.'

Kirstine Hjorth Lorenzen, Noekken Daycare and Waldorf Kindergarten, Denmark, writes:

'We were lucky to move next door to Noekken just before we had our first child. The reason for choosing Noekken had nothing to do with the fact that it was a Rudolf Steiner kindergarten, but more a vague sensation that this place next door had something extraordinary to offer our daughter. Of course our final decision depended on some clarification and exchange of knowledge between Noekken and us. At that point we had not realized the full implications of this decision. Noekken is definitely not just another place where your child is deposited when you go to work.

First of all we were forced to find jobs on reduced time, as our daughter had to be picked up before 2.30 p.m. This was quite a difficult task but we both succeeded, and today we feel very lucky to be working less than full time. Through Noekken we have obtained new knowledge and become much more conscious with regard to such issues as education, health and nutrition. This has been enriching in that we have found many ideas and practices both inspiring and thought-provoking at the same time. One of the results is that we have become more critical and reflective about food, medicine, toys and television. It has been necessary for us to define our own standpoints between the conflicting modes of thought on these issues that we meet respectively "inside" and "outside" of Noekken. This has only worked because the relationship between us parents and the staff of Noekken is based on an openness to discuss issues and a respect for different opinions.

Many of the events which take place depend on the help from parents: the garden and house has to be maintained, cakes and buns have to be made, meetings held, celebrations organized, and so on. Yet all these "duties" are more than just work, as they form a valuable connection between Noekken and the families. One of the results is that we have become quite close friends with many of the other parents, and we have also come to know the staff very well.

What is most important, of course, is that our daughter has had several wonderful years there, with experiences that we also have become a part of. The stability and continuity of Noekken has meant that she has a strong sense of trust and confidence in the place; and all the hours of playing outdoors and the healthy food have contributed to her physical development and well-being. The festivals have provided tremendous joy and enriching experiences.

Most important, though, is the emotional insight and love our daughter has met from the teachers. These personal human attributes are found in other institutions, of course, but it's our conviction that these qualities are especially alive in Steiner education because the teachers have worked with these issues through their training and personal motivation. All this is not to say that the Steiner way is perfect. The qualities and continued well-functioning of this education are dependent on its willingness to discuss different ideas and pedagogical principles and to keep developing its own ideas.'

Margaret Foxweldon, Monadnock Waldorf School, New Hampshire, USA, writes:

'There are people who know they want this education for their children. There are others who "stumble" upon it. We fit somewhere in between. Our neighbour introduced us to the idea and we attended an open house. We were impressed by this education which is imbued with the magic of and reverence for childhood. The philosophy regarding child development made good sense to us, and we liked the idea of educating the whole human being, the hands and heart, as well as the head.

As a Waldorf parent I participate in the festivals, am awed by the solemnity, sparkling light and fragrance of fresh greenery during the Advent spiral, and welcome the spring with music, laughter and dance at May Day. Festivals celebrated in school continue at home, bringing a seasonal rhythm into our family life.

I see and experience the striving of both children and adults, the care and hard work. As the children learn things "deep in their bones", I am encouraged to attend to my own work. I get together with parents to read and discuss, to support each other in our development as adults, parents and home-makers.

Those of us who become "Waldorf parents" are "everyman" – we are single parents, stay-at-home parents, working parents, tired and tireless parents. We have found our way to this education, to the teachers, to the community that works with us to bring to light the goodness, beauty and truth that lives within not only each child, but in all of us. Being a "Waldorf parent" encourages me to be spiritually aware and present in this world rife with distractions of every kind. The challenge, of course, is to take time to re-create this healthy rhythm within my own home, and to be patient with myself and others as we work toward the ideal. Could I have come to the same place without the help of a Waldorf school? Possibly. For me, however, being a Waldorf parent provides a great framework.

Mandy Bell, Gloucestershire, England, writes:

'The first of my three children attended the Waldorf Steiner kindergarten more by accident than design. Following the advice of parents in our new neighbourhood, my daughter and I went along to try out their parent and toddler group. Initially I was totally bemused by how different it was – it didn't fit with my expectations for pre-school education. Not an alphabet in sight! To be honest, I wasn't quite sure about the whole thing.

I think what captivated me was how natural everything was. No pressures on the children to perform, and an environment that was gentle and harmonious. Yet the children still behaved as normal children! My intention had always been for my children to attend mainstream schooling. I had many anxieties in taking the decision that my daughter should remain at the Waldorf kindergarten until after she was five years old, thus missing the entire reception year at primary school. (Here in England, children are increasingly entering school at four.) I knew that she was thriving at the kindergarten, and I felt that she was not ready to move on; but I also feared that she might be left behind educationally and that she might find it difficult to make friends in an already well established group of children.

Seven years on, and my three children are all now thriving both socially and academically in the state system. They all moved into mainstream schooling after the fifth birthday and, consequently, two of them missed the reception stage. I no longer have any doubts about the compatibility of early Steiner education and mainstream education. Neither do I doubt the benefits of delayed entry into "formal" schooling. My children have provided me with all the evidence I need.

Monique Baker, a parent in a Dutch Waldorf School, writes:

'Why did I choose Waldorf education for my children? It is because I so appreciated the atmosphere of the school on my first visit. Seeing the beauty of the classrooms, with the simple toys made of natural materials encouraging imaginative play – it was as if the small child in myself recognized that this was the type of school I wished I had been to! I had read some books on Waldorf education before my children went to the kindergarten. What struck me in these books was that the education is based on a vision of the development of the whole child – not just the mind, but also the body and spirit. Not being an Anthroposophist myself I found many of the ideas expressed in the books puzzling at first, but ultimately valid and helpful after becoming more familiar with them by attending the talks offered for parents at the school, and by seeing them applied in the classroom.

I have found that Waldorf education truly respects, nurtures and protects the developmental stage of the pre-school child, by treating it in a markedly different way to the elementary school child, holding back rather than pushing intellectual development. I especially appreciate the way the naturally religious attitude of the small child is respected and nourished with ideals of beauty, wonder and respect for nature. I was also very happy that at the school I found a whole group of parents sharing the same ideals in raising their children, willing to work together to form a warm and protective environment for them.'

Louise van den Muyzenberg, The Lindens Waldorf Kindergarten, Gloucestershire, England, writes:

'My daughter, Elsa Luna, came to the kindergarten when she was three. It was her first experience of group play and of being away from the family. What she learnt during her time there was to be herself within a group of children. She also learnt the meaningfulness of play. Play as being outside in rainproof clothing, engrossed in mud-pie making or creating "fairy gardens" or planting seeds. Play as in silently listening to a story with other children. Play as in grinding flour to make the bread; felting a small ball with her hands; building and creating little "plays"; using crates and bedspreads and whatever else was at hand. Play as in sharing moments of her life at snack-time. Most of all she enjoyed the love and challenges found in friendship.

What I saw was my daughter growing into herself through play, in a place surrounded by quiet attentiveness, where she was allowed to develop in her own way, without expectations of what she "could be" or "might become". Within her grew a sense of the magic and beauty of the world, of things growing, of creating, of being with others – and of sometimes saying "No!".

Elsa Luna died when she was five years old. Just before she died she wrote down the names of her friends. She was playing with her dolls, telling stories, and singing her favourite songs. They were two important and rich years for her, and with hindsight I could not have chosen a better place for her to enjoy her life.'

From the Teacher's Point of View

Ann Sharfmann, teacher trainer, Centre for Creative Education, Cape Town, South Africa, writes:

'Our work is to prove that Waldorf education can happen in less affluent circumstances, such as the South African township environment. And it does, and it works! Definitely not at all like the European Waldorf kindergarten model, and definitely not yet at all as we want it to be. But we are making a difference in our own small way and we are being noticed.

For us, however, it is the growth and awakening that we see in the children. We have managed to deliver about 30 play-kits to date – a cupboard containing blocks, puppets, felt animals, dolls, cloths, cones, shells, fabrics etc. In many centres the children just sit and look at the toys as they are unpacked. They look and look but do not move. They cannot imagine that such beautiful things are meant for them. When invited to play, they are very hesitant at first, but soon gain in confidence and begin joyfully to play with everything. As you can imagine, even if nothing else changes, being able to play allows these little ones some real childhood activity and they begin to unfold as children. In some classes, where the children have a daily morning ring-time, stories, puppets and the opportunity to draw, model, paint, the difference is astonishing.'

Judith Lee, kindergarten teacher, Orana School, Canberra, Australia, writes:

'It was after more than 20 years of teaching in mainstream education in the area of early childhood and early intervention that I started my journey in Steiner education. More and more in our Australian pre-schools there is a frightening trend to take away children's play time.

In its place children are encouraged to take in as much information as possible, sitting for longer and longer, often in front of computers, and answering meaningless questions. I found that a Steiner kindergarten acknowledges that childhood is a special time and provides a nurturing and protective environment for these years.

In a Steiner kindergarten, children are given time – to use their bodies, grow strong in their limbs, feel secure in daily and weekly rhythms, enjoy all their senses in beautiful surroundings, and imitate adults doing real and meaningful tasks; but more than all this is the wonder and reverence – for seasons, nature and life – that is brought to each child in the day-to-day activities and seasonal celebrations. A Steiner kindergarten acknowledges and supports every aspect of a child's being. It is truly holistic.'

Wiebke Gottschalk, kindergarten trainee, London, and parent and child group leader, Maidstone, England, writes:

To be honest, I never really wanted to be a kindergarten teacher, but it's interesting how life develops sometimes…. I trained as a doctor in my native Germany and took up posts as a Junior House Officer in England. I had just started my General Practice training when I became pregnant with my first child. People always say that having children changes your life, and I couldn't agree more! Suddenly, instead of reading medical journals, here I was studying books on parenting, nursery rhymes and education. The more I read, the clearer it became that I wanted my children to have a Steiner Waldorf education. Luckily enough there *was* a local Waldorf Parent and Toddler Group, but the nearest kindergarten is nearly an hour's drive away.

What is needed is our own Waldorf kindergarten in this area, but for this we need to find premises, funds and – of course – a teacher. But with the growth of the Steiner Waldorf movement in Britain, early childhood teachers are extremely rare. So for me, becoming a teacher wasn't so much a heart-felt wish but a necessity. Saying that, I hasten to add that everything I have read and studied since about Steiner Waldorf education has intrigued and fascinated me more and more. Now, as I write, I am just coming back from the first residential week of my early childhood training course, and I can truly say that I do not regret my decision at all. I am in the right place.

Richard House, kindergarten teacher trainee, London, and toddler group leader, Norwich, England, writes:

'I come from a lengthy academic and psychotherapeutic background; and having worked as a professional counsellor for almost a decade, it increasingly struck me that it would be far more sensible to create a world which minimizes the emotional, spiritual and physical harm done to young children rather than relying on an army of therapists to "pick up the pieces" many years down the line. This realization led me in turn to look into ways of working with young children, and from my soundings there was one approach which stood out above all others – Steiner Waldorf education.

For me the education is underpinned by a love of children, a profound respect for their freedom and a recognition of their inherent wisdom. I found that its world-view and practical pedagogy answered pretty much all of the critical questions I could conjure up about the holistic well-being of children.

I then trained as a Waldorf class teacher (1997-9) and became deeply involved with the founding of a new Waldorf initiative in Norwich. I strongly believe that in working with young children in any learning context, *the quality of presence* of the teacher is crucial; and in my experience Waldorf teacher training is quite unique in directly addressing this most important of pedagogical "intangibles". The education also emphasizes the ongoing *personal development* of the Waldorf teacher – another highly distinctive and invaluable feature of the education.

All in all, it really is a great privilege to train to do this very important work.'

Arunrut Chalermpornpong, Panyotai Waldorf Kindergarten, Bangkok, Thailand, writes:

'I have known Waldorf education since 1997 when I was searching for an elementary school for my children. After reading some books about the education and visiting Panyotai, the Waldorf school in Thailand, I decided to enrol my children there and joined the study group of the school. I soon discovered that this education truly emphasizes the children's inner development, not just simply transferring information from teacher to children. At the time the school was very small and in need of teachers, so I decided to join the faculty. Since then I have realized that Waldorf education is not only positive for the children; as a teacher I am growing with my children and learning equally from them. As a human being it requires me to develop all the time.'

Maria Msebenzi, kindergarten teacher and field-worker, Noluthando Educare Centre, Khayelitsha, South Africa, writes:

'I decided to take the Waldorf kindergarten training because of the needy young souls in our townships. I believe that this type of approach brings us back to our African roots, as human beings in touch with nature – an experience which appears to be fading in the townships. I think this has come about because of the turmoil here.

The culture of story-telling has vanished. Radio and television have taken the place of human relating. The rich story-telling (a true soul sharing) is no longer there. Children are confronted with something that they cannot substantiate or imagine, so they kick and fight for something of a spiritual nature to enrich their souls.

I believe that this type of education is a vehicle for healing the damaged souls of our children. It is quite unique and deepening. The artistic approach of Waldorf education reveals the soul aspect of the human being. By nurturing this seed in our African soil, with this education, I hope that when the roots are anchored in that soil, the plant will have a chance to survive; and that even under the difficult conditions obtaining here, it will eventually bear fruit.

My kindergarten children came to tell me that there was a rainbow in the sky. They said it was beautiful! I never thought that a township child would notice the beauty of a rainbow, much less speak of it... and they notice the flowers too. I can hardly believe it!'

Libby Haddock, kindergarten teacher and parent and child group leader, Monadnock Waldorf School, New Hampshire, USA, writes:

'I have been an early childhood educator for the past 31 years. For the last 18 years, I have been devoting myself to becoming a Waldorf teacher. It has been my experience over these many years that far more than any other form of education with which I have worked, Waldorf education has the possibility inherent within it to help young people develop the strengths and gifts that our twenty-first century world cries out for. We have all endured the disintegration of human relationships, our physical and mental health and environmental pollution. This education truly works at the cutting edge of teaching young people to communicate with one another, to work co-operatively with one another, to love and to care for the natural world in which we live.

We work to help the children build healthy physical bodies. We provide opportunities to learn through creative play, building inner flexibility, imagination and joy. We work to protect the children from being overly stimulated in order that they may learn through their senses. Later in life this develops into the capacity to have healthy relationships with others and with the physical environment. We provide the children with a rich language experience through speech, movement, gesture and song. This helps them to express their feelings and their experiences.'

Shailaja Latchireddy, Hyderabad Waldorf School, India, writes:

'Our school opened its doors in 1996. It started with 23 children in the nursery and kindergarten. I had worked as a teacher for eight years before coming to the school, and I am still surprised that a Waldorf school survives in India – a country of ancient philosophies where spirituality is very much alive. The Waldorf curriculum is based on yet another philosophy, but it has a practical expression that's new in India. At home we do pujas and have numerous rituals. Through Anthroposophy I have begun to understand why we do them. And I am learning to work with my hands!'

Carol Cole, Director of the Children's Program, The Sophia Project, San Francisco, USA, writes:

'For the past four years I have been the director of the Children's Program at Raphael House, a shelter for homeless families in San Francisco. Most of the children (85 per cent) who come to the shelter are five years or younger. Waldorf early childhood education has been the foundation and the inspiration for the work with the mothers and children in both short- and long-term programs.

Waldorf education is rooted in a profound image of the human being. This image is there for each of us, in all its depths, breadth and complexity. Aided by a gradual perception of what it can mean to fully be a human being, the mothers and children can begin to reclaim their human dignity. They can begin to heal.

Closely related to this is the building of relationships. The children and mothers have lived fragmented and isolated lives. Through play, story and artistic activity the children build relationships to nature, colour, music and the whole cosmos. The children and mothers find their place and their connection to the whole. Waldorf education offers an accessible way of building an authentic relationship to life, and this has been a powerful healing force in our work here.

In this education these relationships are built in accordance with the child's stage of development. These stages as set out in Waldorf education have been very valuable, especially in our parent and child work. As we work with the very young child's stage of development, the parents come to value and protect imaginative play because they understand that their child is building inner strength in order to learn to tell his or her own story in the world. They know their child will need this inner strength. The parents can also come to see the power that imitation plays in their child's learning; and through this experience they begin to reclaim the importance of the social environment their child is drinking in so deeply. We have seen these mothers and children begin to reclaim the wholeness of their humanity through their experiences of these aspects of Waldorf education. We are confident that if we take the next step – i.e. developing this work within a strong community framework – the therapeutic and social impact will be enhanced.'

Tina Bruinsma, teacher from Amsterdam supporting the Sloka initiative, India, writes:

'The Waldorf curriculum brings meaning to education. In an Indian context it can de-Anglicize the curriculum and promote the dignity of labour. Teachers and children come to the school with thirteen different mother tongues and seven different religions, and yet this form of education can embrace this diversity. In a country where education has come to mean merely performance, memory and competition bordering on rivalry, a Waldorf school brings with it the deeper meaning behind education.'

Pearce O'Shiel, Waldorf Early Years Training Co-ordinator, the Republic of Ireland, writes:

'The non-denominational or multi-denominational aspect of Steiner Waldorf early childhood education is of particular interest in Ireland. In Northern Ireland, where education has traditionally been divided along sectarian lines, the Holywood Rudolf Steiner School was one of the earliest integrated schools where children from all religious traditions were educated together.

In the Republic of Ireland, Steiner Waldorf early childhood education has been taken up most vigorously in communities which reflect the changing nature of Ireland's population. Many families of Irish extraction are returning to Ireland and, having made a decision to relocate, are looking for new ways of educating and caring for their children, and a renewed sense of community. The fact that Steiner Waldorf education takes as its basis no traditional religious or ethnic rationale, but is derived from what is needed for the development of the child, allows it to speak to people who are themselves searching for what is universally human.'

Regina Hoeck, Waldorf Kindergarten Training Seminar, Moscow, Russia, writes:

'It is my belief that the most important thing that Waldorf education has to offer Russian children is a secure space where they are allowed to be children! Over the past ten years Russia has been shaken by a number of economic and political crises. A "normal" Russian family can survive only if the father has two or three jobs and the mother one or two. Working life consists of constantly having to cope with unforeseen problems.

Russian children visiting Germany were struck most of all by the fact that German mothers have time now and again to play with their children. What Russian children miss most of all is peace and security, rhythm and someone having time for them. On top of this, the state educational system is very intellectual, and formal education at an early age is the order of the day.

A Waldorf kindergarten is often a kind of substitute for the family. In many kindergartens the children stay all day (e.g. 8.00 a.m. to 6.00 p.m.). Here they find security, love and warmth, acceptance in a social group, and grown-ups who have time for them and fill the day with a rhythmic and meaningful programme.

What they find here is the opportunity for creative play and the development of their whole personality through being actively engaged. Here their childhood is secure, and they can gather the forces they will need to cope with the problems they will encounter later in life.'

'The child's brain is soft, his flesh tender. Sun, moon, rain, wind and silence all descend upon him…. The child gulps the world down greedily, receives it… assimilates it and turns it into child.

I remember frequently sitting on the doorstep of our home when the sun was blazing… Shutting my eyes contentedly, I used to hold out my palms and wait. God always came – as long as I remained a child. He never deceived me – He always came, a child just like myself, and deposited His toys in my hands: sun, moon, wind….

Though I did not know this (did not know it because I was experiencing it), I possessed the Lord's omnipotence. I created the world as I wanted it. I was soft dough, so was the world.'

Nikos Kazantzakis, *Report to Greco*

PART II

THE CULTIVATION OF HEALTHY DEVELOPMENT IN WALDORF EARLY CHILDHOOD EDUCATION

Self-initiated creativity brings satisfaction

Chapter 2

Waldorf Education's Distinctive Approach to Healthy Development

Our highest endeavour must be to develop free human beings who are able of themselves to impart purpose and direction to their lives.
Rudolf Steiner

Freedom and Independence

At the heart of education needs to be the fundamental question, 'What is the intention behind this educational experience?'. For Rudolf Steiner, such an intention was inseparable from his image of the human being – and from what is necessary for the release of the developing child's truly human qualities. The central question then becomes 'What does it mean to be truly human?'.

The principles of freedom and independence, which informed Steiner's proposals for social reform (see Chapter 11, 'Our Historical Roots'), are also key features of his image of the human being. These two guiding thoughts – the issue of individual, responsible, freedom and the exploration of our humanity – lay the foundation for Waldorf education.

The practice of Waldorf education approaches learning from two viewpoints: on the one hand, it imparts necessary knowledge and skills to enable a young person to be ready to step out into the wider world; and from the other direction, it releases qualities which will enable her to take responsibility for her own destiny in a self-directing way, from a position of personal well-being.

A Holistic Long-Term Perspective

The success of Waldorf education should be assessed from a wider and more long-term perspective than forms of schooling which judge success more immediately in terms of examination results and achievements in the work-place. An adequate gauging of Waldorf education's benefits would require the evaluation of the quality of life which ex-Waldorf pupils achieve – and their qualities as individuals.

Many factors – home and cultural influences, the nature of the individual child, personal biography – have an influence on personal development. Waldorf education's contribution is the attempt to create a balanced, truly holistic approach to the educational experience, and healthy development is fostered by placing equal emphasis on the strengthening of 'intelligence' in the three forms of human expression – the soul forces of willing, feeling and thinking.

A Developmentally Attuned Education

Waldorf educational psychology also acknowledges that these soul forces of willing, feeling and thinking emerge during certain developmental phases. Timing, or age appropriateness, is considered essential in Waldorf education when deciding what, why, when and how to bring education to the unfolding child. The means of delivering the curriculum, as well as at what age, are given as much consideration as the curriculum itself. Waldorf education also has its own unique curriculum which has evolved from the original indications given by Rudolf Steiner.
Closely and deeply engaged observation reveals how child development progresses in three broad phases, and the Waldorf early childhood phase lays a crucial foundation for the healthy

unfolding of the subsequent phases.

- From birth to seven years the child is most inclined to respond to his world through movement, and is highly sensitive to the impressions which stream from the environment toward his nerve-sense system.

- From seven to fourteen, children live strongly in the emotional realm, and teaching methods which address the feeling life are most likely to arouse the enthusiasm of this age group.

- As the child enters adolescence the realm of ideas and ideals opens up ever-widening horizons.

With these three broad stages of development in mind, the Waldorf early childhood teacher views himself as a support for the will (active) nature of the young child; the class teacher strives to strengthen and deepen 'feeling intelligence'; and the upper school teacher meets the need to experience and explore the world of ideas. (Of course, all three aspects are operative to some extent in each stage of development, but the emphasis varies systematically.) Here, then, we have one of Waldorf education's long-term goals – the eventual healthy interweaving of willing, feeling and thinking in the person's full engagement with life.

The Waldorf curriculum also rests upon an understanding of child development. It is therefore developmentally based rather than subject based. *The content and teaching methods serve the needs of the child rather than the child meeting the demands of a curriculum* – a quite crucial difference.

The teachers strive to be protectors of the sensitivity of early childhood; to be leaders, giving a moral direction and depth to the feeling life in the middle years of childhood; and to be companions in the exploration of ideas and ideals in adolescence.

The desired end-result of this educational experience should be a young adult who is capable of living a positive life from a position of clear thinking ability and a steady, rich, emotional nature – both supported by a strong and active sense of purpose.

An Education for Mind, Body and Spirit

What does it mean to be truly and fully human? The increasing contemporary preoccupation with the physical aspects of our human nature – for example, genetics – deserves our concerned attention, not least in the education sphere. Can the human being be explained fully in terms of 'the physical'? Should the success of education be explained only in terms of the visible and measurable results of academic performance? Different answers to these questions will in turn give rise to very different forms of education.

Waldorf teachers view the child as being a visible, physical entity, possessing an invisible, inner soul life and an eternal spiritual nature. This 'threefoldness' of body, soul and spirit is acknowledged in the content of the Waldorf curriculum, the methods by which it is taught, and in the attitudes of the teachers as they relate to the students. Throughout the school years, the child is recognized as not just the product of her genetic make-up, but also, and equally, as an expression of environmental influences and of her own unique, spiritual nature. The individuality of each child is fostered and, at the same time, strong social skills are encouraged.

A Modern Dilemma

Implicit in Waldorf education is a commitment to defend this conception of the human being from an increasingly materialistic definition of humanity – and against a one-sided view of education expressed in terms of narrowly quantified performance in literacy, numeracy and the sciences. In the Waldorf sphere 'performance' is by no means viewed solely in terms of cognitive intelligence, and the teachers address the longer term implications of their teaching as well as its immediate impact.

Steiner Waldorf education is by no means alone in arguing that our culture's prevailing one-sided definition of 'intelligence' is in need of a quite fundamental review. A so-called 'non-academic' child might well display an admirable 'social intelligence'; an academic 'high-flyer' might fail to 'score' emotionally and leave a trail of unsatisfactory social relationships. The education strives to educate *all* aspects of the individual, in order to open the way for 'success' in all aspects of human endeavour.

Education as Artistic Endeavour

Another fundamental principle is that of infusing all areas of the curriculum with an artistic element. Artistic activity is not seen as something separate but, rather, as a quality which should enter into all areas of the learning/teaching situation. The development of an artistic sensibility in every child is viewed as an essential aspect of the humanizing process. Artistic activity enriches the feeling nature of children and thereby helps to develop their 'emotional intelligence'.

Such a quality has the capacity to warm the intellectual and will aspects of human development and to offset the potential hardness of our physical nature. Rudolf Steiner spoke to this holistic vision of the human being when he referred to 'heart-filled thinking' and 'thinking hearts' as part of our potential as human beings.

Core Waldorf Early Childhood Principles

A respect for education in early childhood is an integral and indispensable aspect of the overall vision of a Waldorf school. Yet Waldorf early childhood education can also be taken as a separate and independent experience, and many parents, through personal choice and circumstance, move their children into mainstream education after the child has attended a Waldorf kindergarten. Experience has proved this to be generally a smooth transition, with the children showing self-confidence, valuable social skills and a natural curiosity toward the learning situation.

The extra time in a Waldorf kindergarten gives them the stamina to cope with the demands of the pressures they frequently encounter when they enter the school situation. But most importantly, they have been given more childhood time!

The kindergarten experience embodies the principles which underpin Waldorf education in general. In broad terms these principles are as follows:

- to provide an experience based upon an understanding of the child's developmental needs;

- to acknowledge children as having physical, emotional, cognitive and spiritual needs; and

- to remain aware of the long-term as well as the immediate effect of the educating process.

In addition, and arising from the latter principles, Waldorf early childhood education has its own specific precepts which are closely attuned to its understanding of the child's developmental needs in the first seven years. These principles are as follows:

- to protect the child's right to a healthy and appropriate childhood;

- to work with, rather than against, the child's natural inclination to be active;

- to use imitation and example as educational approaches;

- to support the child's well-being, and his learning experiences, with the use of rhythm and repetition;

- to provide sufficient time, space and the right equipment for creative play;

- to be aware of the impact of sensory experience in early childhood; and

- to respond to the specific needs of the child's social environment and the times in which we live.

The following chapters illustrate the way in which these fundamental principles are inherent in the Waldorf approach to early childhood education, and describe how they are brought into daily practice within the Steiner Waldorf kindergarten setting.

The need to 'be active' constantly seeks expression

Chapter 3

Movement-based Learning

*...during the first seven years of childhood, the foundation is laid
for the development of a strong and healthy Will.*
Rudolf Steiner, *The Education of the Child*

*It is a morning when the parent and child group (birth to three
years) meets in the room across from the kindergarten (three to
six years). At outdoor time, the two groups share the garden
space, providing an opportunity to observe the changing nature
of the children's movement, from the unsteady steps of the one
year olds to the purposeful activity of the six year olds – and all
the variations in between.*

*A two-year-old girl finds herself beside a small 'pool' that has
been created by the older children in the sandpit. To her
mother's consternation she immediately steps into water – shoes,
socks, the lot! - and then begins to slap the water's surface with
the palms of her hands, sending spray in all directions. Nearby,
some three-year-old boys are digging with spades; they dig with
a wonderful intensity. Although side by side, they are not
working as a team, and there doesn't appear to be a shared,
communal vision of what is being created. A parent walks by
with a watering-can and begins to water a small herb garden.
Immediately the boys drop the spades and move over to join her.*

*The four and five year olds are in the far corner of the garden,
also with spades. The teacher can hear one of them saying 'Let's*

> *pretend that we are farmers and these stones are potatoes. We'll plant them and when they grow we'll sell them'. They begin to make holes in the soil, carefully place a stone in each hole and then cover the holes up. When the teacher returns to the spot 15 minutes later, the stone 'potatoes' are now 'baby turtles' competing in a race.*
>
> *What have the six year olds been doing during outdoor play? They have been huddled together in a corner, chatting and planning; and after considerable teamwork in the 'negotiations', they move off to build a dam – a complex construction involving planks, boxes and stones. This involves a good deal of discussion, co-operation and problem solving, and they're clearly concerned that the dam should work well once they've completed their efforts.*

What have we actually observed in this flurry of activity?

Certainly it is clear that there has been a change in the expression of the children's movement from the age of one through to six. Movement has evolved from what appears to the adults as the seemingly pointless activity of the two year old to the intentional planned activity of the six year olds.

The young child's need to move, and just how this movement can be guided toward self-control, is currently one of the least understood, and least supported, aspects of early childhood development. Instead of self-control, control from 'within', the active nature of children is controlled from 'without' – with children's movement being 'frozen' by television, computers, the demands of the school situation, the needs of adults generally – and, if all else fails, by drugs. Some children accept this situation passively, others protest with disruptive behaviour. This is the immediate effect of our modern misunderstanding. The possible long-term repercussions should also be considered. Society's best interests are surely served by individuals who are able to take initiative, be self-responsible, express enthusiasm, be active – yet in modern culture we appear to be doing everything conceivable, particularly in the educational sphere, to make it virtually impossible for such qualities to emerge and thrive in our children.

How *did* those six year olds become so self-directing, self-controlled, focused; and what does the Waldorf early childhood educator do to bring this about?

The Tiring, Tireless Movement of the Under-Threes

A grandmother was watching her two-year-old grand-daughter moving about the room. 'I get tired just looking at her!', she exclaimed. In parent and child groups, with babies and toddlers (see Appendix 2) there will be many opportunities to observe this early form of movement – apparently random, without purpose, exuberant!

Once a child has overcome gravity and taken that first momentous step, then move they will – endlessly. Movement for movement's sake is joy enough at this age. A consistently still two or three year old is, quite simply, wishful thinking! Their movement is an expression of energy and enviably fresh life-forces. They will need sufficient time, space and opportunity to practise movement under the responsible gaze of the adults who are caring for them.

This need for adult responsibility leads us to a further characteristic of the movement of the under threes. At this stage it isn't yet possible for them to be responsible for controlling their own active nature. They do not possess sufficient consciousness or awareness to become masters of their own movement.

The under-threes are also highly sensitive and attuned to sense impressions. The surrounding environment, with all that takes place within it, immediately affects them and influences their behaviour both positively and negatively (see Chapter 7) The sight of a pool of water is irresistible! It will take a little longer before the two year old can reasonably be expected to hold herself back from the urge to experience the sensation of water on her feet, the effect – and wonder! – of slapping its surface. She will have to be more awake, more conscious, before she can control this type of impulsiveness. (She is not being 'naughty'. She is being a 'normal' two year old.)

The 'Terrible Twos and Threes' – Healthy Defiance!

Toward the end of this phase, movement begins to express itself in a rather volatile form traditionally known as 'the terrible twos and threes'. It wouldn't surprise the teacher if one of the two or three year olds digging in the sandpit were to give a sudden impulsive push to one of his companions, or if two of them were to begin a pushing/pulling contest with one of the spades. Such explosions of will and feeling could well be accompanied by cries of 'No!' or 'It's mine!' or 'I got it first!' – and would almost inevitably end in tears, or in the classic full-blown tantrum.

What is happening? The child is now beginning to realize that it is no longer simply a matter of his own will, but also the complicated business of the will of others in his world – be it mother's will ('You must put on your jacket') or the will of the other children in the group ('I have a right to that spade as well'). It just all becomes far 'too much' at times, and he hasn't yet the inner resources to deal with it in any other way.

'Out of the developing ego springs a tenacious and strident self-assertion which is the opposite of the altruism of imitation.' Jane Girling, 'Child Development in the first 7 years', London Waldorf Early Childhood Training.

Distraction, a rhythmical ordering to his daily routine, opportunity for the imitation of positive and appropriate activities, space for movement – these possibilities will guide him through this perfectly natural phase. He isn't a tyrant, tyrannical as his reign may be at times; and we need to welcome this challenging phase as a healthy and necessary step on his path toward self-identity. He is beginning to awaken to himself as a separate identity, and yet at the same time he is experiencing the demands of being a member of a community (family, playgroup, new friends). This is a difficult enough balance for adults – imagine how it feels for a three year old! It will take some time for him to become accustomed to, and comfortable with, this demanding new experience.

Once the three year old has entered the kindergarten there will be many positive opportunities to capitalize on the natural inclination to imitate. The teacher will continually be aware of herself as an example to be imitated (see Chapter 4). The tendency toward undirected, uncontrolled behaviour is gradually transformed into purposeful, focused activity through the teacher's use of imitation as a teaching tool, and the child's emerging self-mastery. The Waldorf kindergarten teacher will seek ways to guide him toward greater control and attentiveness without force or fear of failure.

The Magical Years: Four- and Five-Year-Old Magicians

The second year of the kindergarten, as the children turn four and five, is notable for the many awe-inspiring expressions of imagination and fantasy through the activity of creative play (see

Chapter 6). The child is now noticeably calmer and has more self-control than when she first entered the group. The clear, rhythmical structure and opportunities for imitation have begun to take effect.

They will have a 'store' of memories of things seen and experienced – trips to the seaside, a ride on a train, the sight of men digging up the road and laying new water pipes, parents preparing a meal. These memories are linked with imagination and fantasy – a type of preparatory thinking – and carry the child into the next phase, as movement begins to express itself in the activity of make-believe – the very heart of childhood.

These are truly magical years and the child is truly a magician. At no other time is movement afforded such a positive, healthy outlet as in imaginative play. Movement is once again purposeful – it has somewhere positive to go. It will make houses, build a train, construct a dam, mix 'cement', enable a child to be a sailor, mother, lorry driver, nurse or bear. A log can be transformed into a drum, table, steering wheel, fiery dragon….

The Waldorf kindergarten teacher now becomes the sympathetic supporter of imaginative play – providing the right equipment, time and space for it to occur. In addition, he will continue to provide opportunities for the child to experience and witness activity which can be added to her store of memories, to be drawn upon as nourishment for play. Puppet shows, stories of high quality, festival celebrations, the image of the teacher's engagement in sewing, cooking, gardening, crafts and maintenance work – life's work – all these activities will be observed and taken in by the children, subsequently to emerge later in their play.

Childhood without Play

In recent years Waldorf educationalists have joined with other early childhood specialists to express their concern that at the very time when children enter this most valuable phase of development, their play is increasingly being 'hijacked', with numeracy, literacy and information technology being presented as substitutes. These academic activities are time-consuming for both child and teacher; and what little time is allocated to play is termed '*structured* play' – the intention being to serve numeracy and literacy goals or some other adult-imposed intention. However, *the instant that play is directed, controlled and made conscious, from outside influences (such as adult intervention), then it by definition ceases to be true play* (see Chapter 6).

A Turning Point:
Idea-based Activity after the Fifth Birthday

In the third and final year of the kindergarten, when the children turn six, they begin to show signs of making a transition from play to school readiness, and the more formal environment which they will enter in Class 1. In the previous year, the will/active forces had linked with imagination and found expression in play. Now they find a new 'partner' – the world of ideas.

The four and five year olds could enter the kindergarten room and, on seeing a number of wooden boxes, planks and a basket of coloured cloths, might well recall a memory of a boat they had once seen. 'Let's build a boat... You can be the captain... I'll be a shark!' is their running commentary as they begin using the equipment to play out the fantasy.

A six year old can arrive at the same solution but via a different route. He is more likely to enter the room, seek out other over-fives and initiate a conversation which will continue for several minutes until an idea emerges. 'I know – let's build a boat.' They will then discuss what they will need to build a ship, seek out suitable materials, negotiate the various roles, discuss potential problems and eventually arrive at the same expression as the four year olds – wooden boxes, planks, basket of cloths. (They might even have had the original idea before they came to the kindergarten and could have been heard in the car saying, 'I'm going to build a boat with Oscar today'.)

Same outcome; different route. The four year old had seen the equipment and then the memory of the boat arose inwardly, stimulated by the sight of the boxes. In contrast, the six year olds first had *the idea* of a boat and then sought a practical solution to building it, involving team work, discussion, planning and negotiation. With the onset of this new, idea-based activity, the teacher perceives that the next phase of development has begun. Movement is now giving a visible outward expression to ideas. This is a valuable foundation for the next step in her education – school-based learning with its call to cognitive activity. The child is preparing to cross the bridge from kindergarten to school.

The Waldorf early childhood teacher now responds by providing many opportunities for these idea-based activities, which has a clear intention before it begins. Weaving to make a bag, sewing to make a doll, woodwork to make a boat, finger knitting to make a rope, plaiting to make a necklace. Not in a contrived way, still not with instruction or compulsion, but in response to the child's expressed need, and using imitation to convey the necessary skills. *Meaning* and *purpose* are now important, and this is an excellent movement-based preparation for the world of ideas which they will increasingly encounter throughout the school years.

A six-year-old girl will join her teacher who is making a doll for the kindergarten and ask if she can make one too – but then go on to produce an entire wardrobe, perhaps even asking to make a bed for the doll. Once introduced to the skill of plaiting, six year olds will sometimes continue for weeks to explore different combinations of colours and different uses for their plaited pieces. The boys will show more interest in activities which involve construction and an enthusiasm to discover how things work.

I observed two boys, who were almost six, spending the best part of an hour constructing a 'castle' with a drawbridge which worked… this was essential! Tables, chairs, pieces of wood – these objects were linked, stacked, upended, and there was a constant exchange of ideas between the two 'builders'. Mechanical laws and the rules of construction were explored alongside fundamental social skills – co-operative working, shared solutions, turn taking, welcoming the contribution of the other. When making a house from stands and bedspreads, the same group will go on to make an extra bedroom, a kitchen, a garden area. Ideas are continually extended, explored and made visible during creative play.

The children experience immense satisfaction and considerable pride in their efforts. In return, the Waldorf kindergarten teacher feels no need whatsoever to signal, in any way, 'This is an incomplete experience. I now want you to make the idea visible on paper', or to coax the child to reflect upon and analyse his achievement. 'How many chairs have you used? How many will you have if I take one away?' Children have many ways of making their statements, most of which are not valued in the current educational climate with its emphasis on the written word.

All the activities described above have been an expression of will.

What do we mean by 'will'?

Children climbing trees, digging in the sandpit, throwing tantrums, expressing themselves in imaginative play; adults at work, striving to strengthen self-discipline, losing self-control when provoked, stilling the mind during meditation. In each example something is active. *Sometimes visibly, outwardly so. Sometimes more inwardly. At times positively, on other occasions, negatively. The force behind this inner and outer activity is* the will.

With young children this will force is unconscious and very potent. With adults, too, the will is at times unconscious, e.g. when driving a car or, more undesirably, in outbursts of violence. But there is also the potential for a conscious will *so powerfully embodied in the statement 'I will!'.*

In The Study of Man *Rudolf Steiner defined the will and outlined its potential for being refined and strengthened with increasing consciousness; from the most basic, physical (body-bound) expressions of instinctive and impulsive behaviour through stages of growing self-awareness of one's behaviour and a longing to take more purposeful, responsible and positive action (a stage of moral development) until we can go beyond the process of self-realization and surrender 'self' to a higher, spiritual expression of the will – from 'I will' to 'Thy will'.*

From the point of view of the will forces, personal development can be seen as the development of the capacity for responsible 'right action' and an increasingly conscious sense-of-purpose. Rudolf Steiner emphasized the essentially human potential for conscious choice and the effect this can have upon the course of our lives. Consciousness is the defining element.

> *For the Waldorf early childhood teacher the challenge is, then: 'How do I work with the unconscious will forces of the child under seven so that these forces gradually become self-directed responses?' There is also the added responsibility arising from accepting that in early childhood '...the foundation is laid for the development of a strong and healthy will'. (Rudolf Steiner)*

The Embodied Will and Physical Care

The forces of will require a healthy body. Children who are tired, frail and generally lacking in energy will not express robust, exuberant will activity. Just as the head is the physical base for thinking, and the rhythmical (breathing, circulation) system the centre for the feeling life, so the limbs provide the physical means for expressing the will. For this reason, Waldorf early childhood teachers take great care to ensure that nothing is done which will weaken or otherwise compromise the child's physical constitution. Warm clothing, organic food, carefully chosen sensory experiences, and a general protective gesture toward the child's physical well-being are central features of the children's care.

The kindergarten teacher is also most careful to resist any kind of 'hot-housing' attitude toward the children in her charge; it is considered crucial that abstract learning and accelerated 'adult-centric' direction do not begin before the child has passed naturally through the transition from play- to idea-based activity, as described above.

Welcoming Movement

It is interesting, and highly revealing, that what was previously referred to as 'hyperactivity' is now more often termed 'attention-deficiency' (ADD or ADHD), marking a shift in emphasis from movement difficulties to attention difficulties. Are we at risk of discriminating against children who resist 'paying attention' in our judging them to be failing in some way? – when 'paying attention' in the way required and expected by the adult world is actually something quite alien and unnatural to this age group who should, in the natural course of development, be exploring their world through movement. This must be especially so for boys!... Or put another way, perhaps children *are* paying attention *through movement* – for the image of those boys 'at work' building the castle with its drawbridge was one of extraordinary attentiveness. (Again, the problem arises as a result of the adult's expectation and definition.)

Place the same age group on seats, require them to 'be still' and attentive to something which at that stage of development is comparatively meaningless – for example, to learn the alphabet – then we shouldn't be the least surprised (or concerned) to find that some of them seem to be 'attention deficient'. On the other hand, the sight of a group of four year olds somehow – and against their nature – managing to be 'quiet and still' is equally disturbing when compared to a group joyfully and enthusiastically taking the initiative to create something from their own will and imagination – and thereby freely offering their attentiveness (something quite unimaginable for many early childhood teachers). After a time, a quality of attentiveness arises quite naturally in children who have been blessed with the opportunity to enter and fully pass through the play-based learning stage of development.

With increasing emphasis on head-based (cognitive) learning in early childhood education, we are witnessing an increasing incidence of movement-based 'dysfunction' or behavioural difficulties in young children. As many early childhood authorities have been arguing for some years, the downward thrust of a subject-based curriculum – as opposed to developmentally informed education – is leading to an increasing emphasis on formal learning at far too early an age.

'The scenario of children, some only just four, who start formal schooling when they are not yet ready to learn is all too familiar to reception-class teachers who are immediately under pressure to get literacy and numeracy hours under way. Young children who have not yet learnt to sit still and to hold their pencils properly (again, it tends to be more boys than girls) resist teachers' attempts to formalise them, and develop all manner of time-wasting strategies, from falling off chairs to running around the classroom.

"A lot of teacher energy is spent in trying to get children to work when all they want to do is move about", says Elizabeth Edgecombe, a former primary school headteacher. Kate Pahl, a researcher at King's College, London, says "One of the problems with the literacy hour is that it requires a lot of sitting on the mat, and that is quite difficult for some boys. Some children are happier to learn kinaesthetically – in a way that involves their whole body – rather than just learning aurally or visually".'

The Independent *Newspaper (UK), September 2000*

A Doing-Intelligence

Waldorf education in early childhood focuses on the strengthening and development of a 'do-ing' intelligence. This involves offering opportunities for experiential learning, a participative learning through personal experience, or implicit as opposed to explicit learning. In other words, learning that is discovered through activity. This type of learning works in harmony with the child's natural inclination toward movement, as opposed to the unnatural imposition to 'be still'. (A four year old reported to her mother that 'the teacher said the girls are good because they sit still but the boys are naughty because they keep getting off their chairs!')

A 'do-ing intelligence' also involves the development of self-control of movement, i.e. also knowing when *not* to move – for example, holding back inappropriate behaviour. This is an important foundation skill that needs to be developed before children enter school.

Waiting for Permission to Move

Parallel to this, we are witnessing an increased use of teacher-directed learning at an early age, with a corresponding reduction in the time and space necessary for child-initiated self-discovery, particularly in the significant realm of imaginative and creative play – and this coming at a time when the child's natural enthusiasm for exploration and experimentation is so vibrant. Based on Steiner's educational philosophy, the long-term effect of this deficiency is predicted to be a weakening of the potential for future self-responsibility and self-direction in the learning process, and in meeting life's challenges generally.

Self-directing, self-responsible individuals – these are two of the long-term intentions of Waldorf education. Is modern educational culture in danger of inculcating a habit of passive dependency, whereby the child waits for direction before becoming actively engaged in his own learning? Or are children being encouraged habitually to seek adult approval in order to substantiate their own efforts?

> ### *Snack-time – the beginnings of a do-ing intelligence.*
>
> *One morning at snack-time, a mixed age group (3-6 years) was gathered around a table. On one side was seated a group of three and four year olds. One boy accidentally fell off his chair and then began to hit his chair, saying 'Silly, silly, chair!'. Immediately, all the other three and four year olds threw themselves on the floor and began banging their chairs, with a great deal of laughter. Across the table, seated next to the teacher (their favourite spot since they had turned six) were two girls. One said 'I want to fall off my chair, but I won't'; and her friend replied, 'So do I. But I won't either!'*

What precisely was revealed in this incident? The three and four year olds had not yet fully mastered movement – they were not yet in the 'driver's seat' in relation to the will forces. They were also easily excited, inclined to lose control, to be carried away by impulsiveness. The pull toward imitation was also very strong.

The six year olds – just two or three years on in their development – were able to control the urge to join the fun, and were also aware of their ability to do so. Moreover, they were able to remain in their seats and continue their snack. This is the beginning of moral activity, or what we term 'good behaviour' – but of a special type. Not good behaviour because of the fear of the consequences, or in order to attract praise (or a gold star) but *self-directed positive responses* to a situation. Because of this awakening ability, the teacher could confidently say, 'These children are now ready for formal learning' – and with equal confidence, 'The four year olds are not quite ready'.

As already mentioned, children are being subjected to early learning before the foundation stage of readiness for learning is completed; and so they enter school before they have the necessary social and behavioural skills which could enable them to cope with the demands of a new and challenging learning situation requiring them to be inactive for a good deal of the time. In this situation, the child experiences anxiety and stress, with the teacher's task being made all the more difficult through having to 'deal with' unready children – altogether a very inefficient state of affairs. Moreover, these are only the immediate effects: the longer-term effects also need careful consideration and research.

Are we in danger of viewing the child's need to be active as 'a bother'? In the light of these disturbing trends, the active quality of the Waldorf kindergarten is beginning to be seen as having a crucial *therapeutic* task for a generation of children who have been effectively 'immobilized' – by a culture dominated by, for example, television, computers, adult preoccupation with their safety, precocious intellectual activity and so on.

The early childhood teacher can provide opportunities for children to develop the habit of *taking action* – a love of action which Rudolf Steiner referred to as the fundamental principle of education in early childhood. The children will have a further habit, the habit of self-direction, and through creative play will have discovered the joy of creativity, the habit of seeking creative solutions to the challenges they meet, to be able to imagine alternatives – a much-needed quality for the times we live in.

Do Children *Only* Play in Waldorf Kindergartens?

Working with young children in this active way requires teachers to be comfortable with a certain degree of creative chaos! However, having followed this approach to working with children in early childhood, the teacher must also consider certain important questions. If children are allowed to remain only 'in action' and only to practise 'self-direction', and if the will forces are allowed full, uninhibited reign, then a dangerous imbalance will occur. The will forces, of course, also have the potential to overwhelm the child, to become chaotic, destructive, to 'run wild'; and the love of self-direction and the experience of autonomy that accompanies it can readily descend into self-interest. A balance between freedom and form must be achieved.

How can we bring an ordering to the active nature of the child so that it is guided in a positive direction and remains within acceptable boundaries? How can we balance self-confidence and self-assertion with a sensitivity toward the needs of others?

The Waldorf early childhood teacher has two educational 'tools' which can answer these challenges. They are the use of *imitation and example*, and of *rhythm and repetition*.

The child reveals a trusting willingness to imitate the adult-world

Chapter 4

Learning through Imitation and Example

*There are two magic words which indicate how the child
enters into relation with his environment: they are
Imitation and Example*

*...Physical environment must, however, be taken in the widest
imaginable sense. It includes not only what goes on around
the child in the material sense, but everything that takes
place in the child's environment.*

Rudolf Steiner, *The Education of the Child*

'An Absolute Necessity to Imitate...'

Most educational activity involves the teacher offering an example
to some degree. These examples will be supported by direction
and instruction to convey the aim and content of a lesson.
Listening to an authority is an appropriate method for school-age
children. In the first seven years, however, the child is naturally
inclined to imitate, and to be active; and for this reason the
Waldorf kindergarten teacher relies almost entirely upon example
as an educational approach, confident that the children will follow
her through their natural imitative response. The imitation of a
worthy example is an appropriate method for early childhood
education and this approach is both practical and effective.

Surrounded by children whose stage of development means
almost constant movement, the teacher acts as a focus, a centre-
point, around which this movement finds direction. The teacher

works *with* movement rather than attempting to restrain it. In his book *The Way of the Child*, A. C. Harwood writes, 'It is useless to tell them not to touch, not to taste, not to move, not to meddle. They do what they will. But in the heart of this apparent lawless age, nature has inserted a law of authority. Young children are bound by an absolute necessity to imitate.'

Why Imitation?

The child under five is extremely open and highly sensitive to all that flows toward him from his surroundings. These qualities of openness and sensitivity combine with the inclination to respond with movement - and the result is the act of imitation. Imitation is a union of impressions coming toward her from the outer world and the child's inner world of will. He sees and then he does. He is not able to distance himself from, or remain unaffected by, what he experiences in the same way as an older child or adult.

Imitation and Example versus Explanation and Direction

Why is it that imitation and example are considered more desirable than explanation and direction at this age? Since the 1960s it has become increasingly common practice for both parents and teachers to use a more intellectual approach with young children, involving questioning, choice, explanation and instruction. With their particular sensitivity (see Chapter 7), this 'bombardment' pulls young children into an accelerated consciousness. A 'hyper' quality is usually the result, both in their speech ('verbal hyperactivity') and in their behaviour. Many children have a precocious self-awareness and self-consciousness; they have become 'little adults'. In this sense, the use of imitation and example as a teaching method constitutes a non-intellectual approach which is able to reach the naturally dreamy, not-fully-awake consciousness of the unspoilt child before the fifth birthday. This approach thus works with the natural pace of the child's development rather than accelerating and inducing qualities which are more natural to the over-sevens.

Drawing upon both theoretical insight and practical observation, kindergarten teachers believe the use of imitation and example to be an age-appropriate learning method. Cognitive-based learning is avoided in favour of a movement-based self-initiated experience (imitation). This approach then lays the foundation for a lifelong capacity for self-discovery.

At the end of three years in a Waldorf kindergarten, the child has literally developed the habit of taking initiative – a 'love of action'. This capacity proves to be an enormous asset later in life, particularly if this healthy foundation is not undermined later in the educational process.

Trust and Respect

The seizing of the opportunity to imitate in early childhood demonstrates a willingness to follow an adult's lead, without being coerced to do so. This too becomes habit, and an attitude of respect and trust for the adult world is fostered through this experience. This is an important step for moral education, and can prove to be a valuable preparation for the school years when the Waldorf class teacher will require the children to follow him in many ways.

Waldorf teacher training constantly emphasizes the importance of self-education and self-development for the teacher, so that the role of being the 'example' is met with responsibility and is worthy of the child's trust and respect.

Imitation – a Willing Response

Imitation cannot be taught. It arises naturally from within the child and each child will imitate in his own uniquely individual way. There is a wonderful, subtle balance involved in the act of imitation. On the one hand it is an activity of individuality – the child is choosing to do something, rather than being instructed to do it. On the other hand, it is also a willingness to join another individual, to empathize – *an 'I and you' experience*, a healthy swing between 'me' and 'we'. This has implications for the development of positive social skills, whilst at the same time self-identity and self-esteem are fostered. This can be described as a healthy egoism, or ethical individuality, a quality of increasing significance in the times we live in.

The problem of being both an individualist and also a member of a community is a very modern challenge, and Waldorf education begins to help children to deal with this in the kindergarten, with valuable social skills thereby being learnt before they enter school.

As a general principle we can say that *the act of imitation 'softens' self-assertion without damaging self-esteem.*

Three Levels of Imitation

Imitation functions on three levels:

* *A child sees, and immediately imitates*
  This is the most simple and obvious form of imitation. Every morning the children will arrive at the kindergarten to find the teachers actively engaged in some form of activity – painting, modelling, domestic activity of many kinds – a wealth of activities which immediately arouse the interest and enthusiasm of the younger children. The child is not obliged to

join the activity, but he inevitably does so. The most common response is 'Can I do it too?'. The child is freely volunteering his co-operation! (Parents will, of course, recognize this situation. How often do we begin to wash a car or bake a cake, for example, to find ourselves being asked the same question?)

* ***The child sees, and later imitates***
This 'delayed' form of imitation can be continually observed during creative playtime. In fact, play is an expression of constant imitation. A child who has seen his father using a cement mixer may, a few days later, or even weeks later, re-enact this in the garden using sand, water and spades, often with uncanny accuracy, even down to the corresponding gestures. I have observed a four year old continue for weeks to imitate the building of road-works outside her house. On another occasion I found a five year old placing a plank across two logs and then pushing boxes, one after the other, across the plank with an accompanying whirring noise. I discovered he was re-creating the sight of the luggage conveyor belt which he'd seen at the airport on his way to Lanzarote!

Sometimes the children will re-play a story they've heard, or a simple domestic scene such as putting a baby to bed or making a meal, or imitate the voice and mannerisms of a playmate. This form of imitation can also provide healing opportunities. A child whose older brother had died re-enacted the funeral service many times with her doll and in this way came to terms with the event, in a way that she could not achieve intellectually. Imitation is one way in which young children can come to terms with events in their lives, and integrate them in a healthy way.

* ***The child sees and gradually 'becomes'***
This is a more subtle, yet powerful, form of imitation. It is an

'inner imitation' with long-term implications. It calls for considerable responsibility from the adult world, for children also absorb attitudes, moods, habitual responses. These begin over time to influence the person he will become. He is imprinted with the moral values of his community.

A young child will, of course, imitate both positive and negative images. Images on television, in computer games, the behaviour of adults and other children – these all make their mark. The acceleration of violent children's behaviour – children killing children, as in the recent American school 'shoot outs' – begs us to give responsible consideration toward deciding just what images we choose to place before our children.

The Teacher as Example

The Waldorf teacher expects to accept responsibility for what the child is exposed to in the kindergarten environment, and willingly acts as a guardian on the threshold between the child and outer influences which form her image of what it is to be truly human. As mentioned in the previous chapter, Waldorf teacher training emphasizes the personal development of the teacher as the foundation upon which her work will stand. Teachers can ask the question, 'What type of example am I?'. A possible answer might be – an example of someone who is striving to become a balanced, healthy, human being. Not perfect, but striving!

If a child is to move toward self-control he must first experience and observe self-discipline in adults. Children begin their life in a mood of trust and teachers need to be responsible toward this trust.

Today there is so often a dramatic, hyperactive quality to many children's lives. Their delicate, sensitive nerve-systems are constantly stimulated and overloaded at an increasingly early stage in their development. Little wonder that hyperactivity is reflected (or perhaps imitated?) in their behaviour, which is then labelled as 'difficult'. Sadly this 'difficult' behaviour is increasingly controlled by drugs such as Ritalin.

Healthy children, undamaged by over-stimulation and premature intellectuality, are naturally willing to become apprentices to a teacher's many skills. In the act of imitating positive, appropriate, meaningful activity beside a calm, well-organized and understanding teacher, a young child is allowed to learn these new skills in an undemanding, non-exhausting way. The child's volition is offered an opportunity for orientation and he is led toward *self*-control rather than being *drug*-controlled.

Working with Imitation in the Kindergarten

Being in a stage of development characterised by activity and creativity, children will be most attracted to adults who are themselves visually active, visually creative. Throughout the morning all the adults in the room will continue to be busily involved with work that needs to be done, avoiding all abstract activity which has no real significance for the child of this age. The daily work of preparing the meals, caring for the environment, mending, making and cleaning – all offer sufficient opportunity for the learning of new skills and a positive direction for young will forces. This age group enjoys all manner of domestic activities, and in the process learns the many skills involved in domestic science – chopping, measuring, pouring, weighing... The image of the teachers at work acts as a magnet for the children; and the teacher will be well prepared so that everything is in place to enable the children readily and easily to join her in the work.

In an age where many mothers are working outside the home and may be unable to offer such opportunities in the natural home environment, such an experience in the Waldorf kindergarten becomes increasingly valuable.

At ring-time the principles of imitation and example become particularly significant as the teacher becomes aware of the influences of her own speech and gesture. From the more open, child-initiated activities of creative play, the ring-time becomes a teacher-led moment in the morning. Using appropriate seasonal themes, for example, an imaginary walk through a wood in autumn, sowing and harvesting wheat in late summer, the teacher becomes a source of knowledge and understanding of the world, of vocabulary, clear speech, control of movement, imagination, listening skills, phonological awareness – all through the clear and conscious example that she presents. These skills lay a solid foundation for literacy and numeracy at a later stage.

This daily teacher-led moment prepares the way for the acceptance of the Waldorf class teacher's authority in the school years. The teacher has become a clear point of reference, and the children are encouraged to balance the individual freedom of creative play with the communal, co-operative mood of ring-time, whilst at the same time looking toward the teacher as leader. We can see in this instance how the skilful use of imitation and example has the capacity to develop social skills. They are also extremely effective as a means of bringing about positive behaviour, a creative form of non-authoritarian discipline.

Consolidating the Positive Effects of Imitation

Working daily with this approach, then, the Waldorf teacher now has a further educational 'tool' which will work in partnership with the principle of imitation.

Whilst the imitative response is a constant theme throughout the Waldorf early childhood programme, certain moments in the day regularly involve imitation and will be repeated on a regular basis. A *rhythmical repetitive element* in the kindergarten experience thus brings another dimension to the use of imitation and example. We now need to consider the place of *rhythm and repetition* in the Waldorf kindergarten.

Children need the time and space for the wonder of discovery

Chapter 5

The Use of Rhythm and Repetition to Support Learning and Healthy Development

For this is a great secret: all the healing forces reside originally in the human breathing system.

Rudolf Steiner, *Four Seasons and The Archangels*

The Waldorf nursery or kindergarten looks effortless; it looks as if the teacher isn't doing very much. Up to twenty children play harmoniously and move from one activity to the next throughout the morning without the teacher having to stop to solve major problems or interruptions. While it may look easy, a great deal of preparation has gone into creating an environment that fits the children and planning a rhythmical series of activities that allow freedom of movement within a structure that holds and supports the children.

Rahima Baldwin, *You Are your Child's First Teacher*

The word 'rhythm' evolves from the Greek word 'ruthmos' meaning 'to flow'. This derivation encapsulates the intended mood of the Waldorf kindergarten experience from the child's point of view. The children are guided by a smooth, soothing, flowing, logical quality inherent in the progression of each aspect of the morning, and careful thought will be given to the transition moments between one activity and the following. This creates a quite different atmosphere from a 'timetable'.

Short-, medium and long-term planning are represented in the kindergarten by day, weekly and yearly rhythms, and these rhythms are repeated so that the child soon becomes reassured and led by the consistency of her experience each time she returns to the kindergarten. What is required of her becomes self-evident as a result of the carefully structured environment, in which rhythm has a type of 'innate authority' for the child.

A visitor will soon become aware that there is a distinct rhythmical quality to each session, and that the morning's pattern consists of two major 'waves' of contraction and expansion.

Creative Play - *expansion* . . . . . . the child breathes out;

Circle Time - *contraction* . . . . . . the child breathes in;

Outdoor Play - *expansion* . . . . . . the child breathes out;

Story Time - *contraction* . . . . . . the child breathes in.

The times of expansion are marked by child-initiated activity and make up the longer span of time at this stage of the child's development. The moments of contraction are teacher-led times. In this way the child's experiences are brought into a healthy balance. He does not remain too long in self-expression; nor does he remain too long within the restriction of communal moments.

The rhythm soon becomes habit, and very quickly these habits are established and become unquestioned, removing the need for instruction and direction. The child literally 'goes with the flow'.

A Typical Daily Rhythm

Although each teacher is free to establish her own rhythmical pattern according to the needs of her situation, the principles of contraction and expansion will remain. A typical daily rhythm might be as follows:

9.00 - 10.00   ***Creative play*** *and daily activity (see next box)*

10.00 - 10.30   *Tidy-up time and* ***circle time***

10.30 - 11.00   *Wash hands and snack time*

11.00 - 12.00   ***Outdoor play***

12.00 - 12.30   *Preparation for story time;*
                 Story time or puppet show;
                 Goodbye

The Weekly Rhythm

The daily rhythm will continue while the weekly rhythm is marked by the teacher's choice of daily activities which will be offered within the creative play time. (Please refer to the reading list for books which will give a detailed explanation of the various artistic activities in Waldorf kindergartens.)

For example:

Monday   Painting with watercolours, *which allows the child to take pleasure in the easy movement of the brush, the flow and interaction of the colours.*

The child's pleasure is in the doing and the experience rather than in the result. Her artistic sensitivity is developed in this way.

Tuesday   Beeswax crayon drawing *when the child can find satisfaction in the more forming quality of the crayons.*

Wednesday   Modelling with beeswax*: the child can experience herself as a 'creator' and discover naturally the principles of form. The smell and tactile quality of the beeswax add another dimension to the experience.*

Thursday   Bread-making and soup-making, *through which the children discover* process – *the grinding of wheat, mixing, kneading, spreading, eating. They also meet technology and science in a meaningful context – e.g. the grinders and the oven.*

Friday   Cleaning day*: in polishing, washing, ironing, sorting, sweeping, they come to learn to respect and care for the environment. (This general caring quality of the Waldorf kindergarten shows its effect in the social sphere.)*

The opportunity for handwork and craft activities, related to the seasons and the celebration of the seasonal festivals, will also be offered within the creative play time.

The Yearly Rhythm

This will be conveyed through the experience of the seasons, which is an important element in Waldorf early childhood education. The celebrations of the festivals stand as beacons across the cycle of the year, and the seasons find reflection in the teacher's choice of song, verse, story, domestic and artistic activities, as well as her decoration of the environment. A seasonal 'garden' will evolve throughout the year in harmony with what is happening outside in nature. All activities – handwork, craft, domestic work – will have a connection to something in the prevailing season, enabling the children to form a living relationship to the passing of time through the year's cycle.

Wherever possible the outdoor play space will be designed to give the children direct contact with seasonal changes, and the possibility for season-linked activities, such as gardening and the growing of plants which can then be used in activity – lavender for lavender bags, rose-hips for rose-hip syrup, vegetables for soup-making, calendula flowers for the dyeing of fleece. These activities will also have a clear rhythmical repetitive quality, returning each year in the same season and creating much-loved traditions.

The celebration of the festivals is a significant part of the kindergarten programme. Parents are involved in these communal gatherings, and the children gain a sense of 'belonging', of being embraced by a wider circle of caring adults where wonder and reverence are fostered. (It is beyond the scope of this book to do full justice to this important aspect of kindergarten life, so the reader is encouraged to explore the meaning and celebration of festivals in the books recommended in the reading list.)

How deeply this use of rhythm enters the child is demonstrated in the following incident. An assistant worked only three days a week, and on Tuesdays she always baked the bread with the children. One Monday a child mistakenly called the group leader by this assistant's name. Another child called out 'Don't be silly; it can't be Clare – this isn't bread-making day!'. Teachers frequently tell stories of how children will arrive and ask, 'What day is it?', and are puzzled if the teacher replies 'Wednesday' because they are expecting the reply 'soup-making day' or something similar.

Other Rhythms within the Kindergarten Day

The structuring of time is an obvious example of rhythmical activity. The rhythmical principle is extended to all aspects of the kindergarten. A snack will be served on a particular day – for example, muesli on Tuesdays, soup on Wednesdays... The following examples demonstrate the versatility of this particular educational principle.

The rhythm of 'how things are done'

Many daily moments require the teacher to decide what is the best way to do something, from the child's point of view. Having made this decision, this chosen way will be repeated daily and will become habit: the way in which children will be called to circle time, how the table will be set, the beginning and ending of the story time, how the children prepare themselves for baking (washing hands, putting on an apron), and so on. In this way the children learn, without undue pressure, how things are to be done.

The rhythm of 'where things are kept'

Nothing is more frustrating for a child than to be in the middle of imaginative play – perhaps building a 'bakery – and to discover he needs a piece of wool to tie the 'walls' together... only to find that the basket of wool pieces is no longer on the shelf where it had been the day before! For this reason, equipment in a Waldorf kindergarten is openly displayed, and the teachers are very conscious of the need for each and every item to have its place. This also enables the child to move independently, to take the initiative in fetching what she needs. It also allows her to co-operate at clearing time, for she will know 'where things live'. At such a young age children themselves are 'dis-ordered', and this atmosphere of order helps to settle the will forces.

The rhythm of 'response'

The experienced Waldorf teacher will soon build up a selection of responses to the most common situations that arise during the course of the kindergarten morning. If a child uses his hands to hit or push another child, one teacher might always say 'Hands are for work and play'. These responses are not, of course, written in stone; rather, each teacher will develop these rhythmical responses according to what she personally feels comfortable with – the important point being that they are appropriate to the child's stage of development, and are repeated. The children come to accept them and so unpleasant and exhausting negotiations are avoided.

There will be other such examples of rhythmical activity, and it is important to emphasize that this aspect of the work is open to the fresh creativity of each teacher.

The Significance of Rhythm for the Healthy Development of the Child

In his series of talks to the teachers in the first Waldorf school, Rudolf Steiner referred to the need 'to teach the child to breathe rightly'. This statement needs to be taken in the widest sense, and on a number of levels, but the general implication is the need to introduce a 'breathing-like' quality into the child's daily life – to live as we breathe.

One way of defining 'rhythm' is as a flow between a state of contraction (breathing in) and a state of expansion (breathing out). In the act of contracting, be it resting, meditating or reading, we return to ourselves and gather strength. We are still. We reunite with our sense-of-self and experience 'centredness'. We gather ourselves back inwards and turn toward our inner spiritual nature. When we expand, we go out to meet the world, revealing our social, communal, interacting nature. We are active and expressive; and we demonstrate an interest other than self-interest.

Our physical and emotional well-being depends upon a balanced interplay between the polarity of contraction and expansion. If we remain too long in a state of introspection we become isolated, self-absorbed, turned in upon ourselves. On the other hand, if we dwell too long in outward-seeking activity, we become formless, unravelled, unsteady. Once conscious of this need, adults can choose to create this healthy balance in their daily existence. But this balance is beyond the informed, conscious choice of the young child, and so the responsibility for this element in their lives belongs to the adults who care for them. Waldorf education rests firmly upon this rhythmical principle.

Implications for Health

An essential thought for the Waldorf early childhood teacher is that the will forces require a 'home' in a healthy body. As mentioned in Chapter 3, everything will be done to protect the child's physical health, and rhythm has the potential to support health and preserve the strength of the child's life forces.

In a world in which the incidence of asthma and allergic reactions in early childhood is inexorably rising, the healing, soothing, untiring qualities of a rhythmical ordering of the child's day is an important and easily achieved 'environmental antidote' to these disturbing trends. Similarly, in this way, the child's overall stamina is strengthened and delicate children are particularly protected.

Bringing Order to Impulsive Behaviour

The will forces of the young child can be overpowering and the child can be 'blown away' by this force. The ordering potential of rhythm gradually guides the child's movement and contains his energy until such time as he can himself be the guide.

Rhythm helps the child to 'take hold' of her physical body. As Steiner commented, 'You direct the impulse of the will aright, not by telling a child once what the right thing is, but by getting him to do something today and tomorrow and again the day after'. This early experience of order and regularity is the seed for future self-discipline.

Bringing Order to Feelings

The flow between 'out breath' and 'in breath' in a daily rhythm helps children to steady their emotional responses. Even adults can experience how volatile feelings become when they are tired! Rhythm can help the child to handle frustration, to find a 'way forward' for her feelings. The next step is self-evident.

In the popular book *The Road Less Travelled*, Scott Peck begins with an exploration of the fundamental need for children to experience delayed gratification as a foundation for later self-discipline. Our children live in an 'I want it now!' culture, and immediate gratification has become habit for so many of them. The use of a rhythmical ordering of their experiences from the earliest years signals, 'No, you must wait: this has to happen first'.

In the kindergarten, waiting for the candle to be lit before eating begins, singing a song before the story can be heard, washing hands and putting on an apron before you can help with the bread-making – small 'doses' of delayed gratification strengthen self-control without resorting to bribery, threats or punishment.

Supporting Learning

Rhythm also allows young children to learn rhythmically that which would be difficult to learn conceptually at such a young age. A repeated activity allows even a two year old to learn new skills without coming into a more intellect-based consciousness for which he is not yet quite ready. Memory is strengthened in this easy, effortless, non-failing way. For this reason, stories, verses and songs are repeated over a number of days.

Rhythm by its very nature has an innate logic – it has a natural order. The child is able to grasp a logical sequence in these repeated events. These qualities address his conceptual cognitive abilities in a way that is manageable at his stage of development.

Waldorf teachers will make every effort to ensure that everything they do in front of the child is done in a logical, naturally progressive, ordered manner. The children are able to pick up the 'clear signal' and, additionally, will find it easy to imitate the activity. The self-discipline of the teacher is acknowledged as an essential prerequisite for the children's eventual self-control.

Instilling Trust

Many children today are in situations where they are 'prematurely awakened' to a wider world, with its adult preoccupations, expectations and possibilities for danger; and as a result they are often very caught up in the dramatic quality of the adult world. Their in-born trust is frequently shaken by the inconsistencies in their lives: Is daddy leaving? Who will pick me up? Where are we going now? What am I supposed to do? When will mummy be home from work?...

Anxieties can and do gradually ease, however, as the kindergarten's daily and weekly rhythms lift from the child the burden of wondering what will come next, what will be expected of her. The steady, returning rhythms of the kindergarten are particularly healing for children in difficult circumstances. They signal to the child: *'Here you are safe and you can trust in what you'll find here.'*

Let's pretend...creative play is the very heart of childhood

Chapter 6

Creative Play: Why Is It So Vital?

*There is only one difference between the play of the child
and the work of the adult. It is that the adult adapts himself
to the outer utility which the world demands; his work is
determined from without. Play is determined from within,
through the being of the child, which wants to unfold.*

Rudolf Steiner, Dornach lecture, 1923

---

*Once upon a Tuesday morning, Barnaby (aged 4) began to
place a row of bricks about 30 centimetres out from the wall.
This line of bricks continued around the four sides of the room.
He then returned to the first brick and set about balancing
planks against the outside of the row of bricks. Once this activity
was completed, he ran a long line of rope around the entire
construction, between the bricks and the wall. At the end of this
operation, Barnaby came to his teacher and exclaimed – with a
huge grin of pleasure and satisfaction – 'I'm the builder. I've put
in new central heating for the kindergarten!'*

---

*Once upon a Friday morning, Elsa and Paloma (aged 4 and 5)
set up house. Wooden play-stands formed the outer walls and a
bedspread served as a roof. Inside, an upturned box became a
cooker, a bowl served as a saucepan, and a handful of conkers
was accepted as potatoes. 'Let's pretend I'm the mother and you*

are my little girl', said Elsa. Lunch was prepared, they went shopping, and a general atmosphere of domestic purpose prevailed. Suddenly, a knock on the door: 'Can I play too?', asked Megan. 'The house isn't big enough for three people', replied Elsa. Megan was clearly disappointed. The teacher's advice and support were then sought. 'Megan could be a friendly neighbour', suggested Elsa. 'That's a good idea. We could share an allotment!', exclaimed Paloma. An adjoining house was quickly constructed with the help of Elsa and Paloma, and Megan took up residence, proving to be a very friendly neighbour indeed. Some 15 minutes later, the teacher observed that the house had now become a hospital, since Paloma 'had hurt her foot when working on the allotment' and Elsa and Megan were now nurses. The injured foot had been bathed and bandaged, and the conkers were now 'remedies'.

Once upon a sunny day, Jo and Theo (aged 6) were digging in the garden in an area slightly elevated above the kindergarten's vegetable plot. They began to dig trenches. At first these were random, until Jo began to direct the trench, digging toward the vegetable garden. When they reached the low stone wall which separated the two areas, they began to dig downwards until they reached the spot beneath the stones. They then found a way to dig beneath the stone wall and to find an exit on the other side and out into the vegetable plot. Theo then proceeded to fill a watering-can from the nearby tap and to pour the water into the opening of the trench. The result – an impressive irrigation system.

Once upon a morning, not long after Christmas, two five year old girls announced, 'We miss Christmas and want to make a

Christmas tree'. But neither a Christmas tree nor a branch of greenery in sight! They pulled a box to the centre of the room and placed a plank on top. Then another box, and another plank on top. A tower form was emerging, and a group of interested children had gathered around the purposeful activity. One observed that 'It doesn't shine like a Christmas Tree'. After some debate a child offered the solution of placing a lit lantern on top of each plank, before then placing a further box on top of it. Another child was dispatched to ask the teacher to help provide a number of enclosed lanterns. The challenging task of building up a tower-like version of a Christmas Tree soon became a team effort, with four year olds playing the part of 'fetchers', the five year olds carrying out the complicated construction work, and the six year olds providing instruction and a general running commentary.

When the completed construction stood as a shining symbol of a triumph over adversity, it was announced that decorations were required. Fortunately, the teacher always kept a shoe box of decorative bits and pieces, and soon this unlikely apparition was festooned with ribbons, coloured wool, straw stars, small wooden toys, and – last but certainly not least – a doll was balanced precariously on the very top. There it was – a huge, twinkling, wooden Christmas Tree; and all that was left to do was to stand and gaze in wonder and to sing carols.

Every Monday morning, five-year-old George, a child with severely delayed speech and communication difficulties, entered the kindergarten and went straight to the cradle where his favourite doll lay. He would then tenderly caress and kiss the doll, bring it to the teacher for a hug, and then proceed to carry

> *the doll with him throughout the morning. The teacher observed that the doll drew from George important emotional responses – tenderness, imagination and attempts at non-verbal communication. At story-time he was encouraged to bring the doll with him, and this enabled him to listen to the story, whereas previously he had tended to go 'out of himself'. The hugging of the doll drew him back from the periphery, and consequently he was able to experience himself as a centre-point. This imaginative activity was gradually awakening George's sense of his own identity – an important stage if he was to proceed to gain control over his speech.*

Play under Siege

Childhood without play seems inconceivable... or does it? Adults work, children play... or do they?

Inappropriate early childhood practice in the form of a downward thrust of literacy and numeracy performance and assessment continues relentlessly to erode the boundaries of early childhood. Five year olds are expected to perform as six year olds had previously performed, and four year olds are met with the challenges previously presented to five year olds.

Parents frequently describe their four and five year olds as 'coping' rather than 'flourishing' in the early years of school experience. One significant sacrifice to this trend is the child's access to the world of creative play. The willingness of educational policy-makers to dismantle and undermine this activity is due, in part, to a rapidly disappearing understanding of the nature of play and its contribution to later achievements and development.

What Is Play?

Once upon a time... Let's pretend... You be... and I'll be... With these words children take a step into a world without boundaries, rich with potential learning opportunities, and an essential stage in their development. Observe children play. Watch and listen. Be prepared to be astounded by what you will see and hear.

The child's need to play must first be acknowledged. The adult's work presents itself from 'outside'; the child's play arises from 'within' as an impulse to integrate her experiences. 'The child needs his will-reaction, his play, in order to assimilate his experiences and make them fully his own' (Rudolf Steiner).

Here is an example. The older brother of a four-year-old girl had died. The day after the funeral she began to make a mound of blankets and pillows into which she burrowed. These were the 'clouds' and she was going in 'to bring her Jacob back'. Teachers working in areas of deprivation – war-torn environments – will observe children literally 'playing out' their anxieties, with a corresponding easing-up of tension as they come to terms with their situation through the activity of play. Play therapy is a standard practice for professionals working with abused children. When a child is unwell, play activity will cease; its return will signal that the child is well again.

A child at play is a child at peace.

> '...children are also dreamers. There is something almost spiritual in the imagination of a child, who picks-up bits and pieces of its surroundings and its memory and finds out how they fit together in a slow, dreamlike process of discovery. They

don't do this playing a computer game. They do this when they are allowed to sink down into themselves… they do it when they have time. Time is what we have taken away from children.

Nicci Gerard, The Observer, 6th August 2000

Misunderstanding the Nature of Play

The inner source of play decisively undermines a growing contemporary trend toward 'structured play' in early childhood settings. This concept of directing play from 'outside', with an imposed intention – for example, to develop a concept of the number '5' through the use of five teddy-bears having a picnic – fails in any way to meet the true definition of play, which must, *by its very nature*, arise from within the child and have no purpose other than to satisfy the original impulse. This impulse might arise from the need to 're-play' the image of men laying water pipes, or to come to terms with physical abuse. It might arise from the need to 're-live' a fairy-tale told by the kindergarten teacher – or simply, once again, to experience what Steiner described as the joy and intensity of 'the love of action'. For play is also a will activity and a further revelation of the extent to which young children are impressed by their environment; for it is also an act of imitation.

The inner need to play breaks through – and makes bearable – the most deprived circumstances in which children find themselves. Ute Craemar (see Brazil report in chapter 9) has described a young boy taking a rusty tin from a tip and beginning to strum it like a guitar.

We need to be clear that play is a strong, developmental, inner need, and ceases to be authentic play when it is manipulated from outside the child according to another's agenda.

Changing Consciousness and Its Effect upon Play

There are further conditions which need to exist in order for play to arise from within the child. We need to understand the quality of consciousness which gives birth to play activity. Just as the child undergoes physical changes – becoming taller, acquiring more physical skills – so too does her consciousness or 'awakefulness' evolve. This evolving consciousness can best be understood if we relate it to the states of being asleep, dreaming or being fully awake. These stages of awakefulness in the human being find counterparts in the different stages of early childhood development.

The new-born infant spends a good deal of each day literally asleep; and when he is awake, his consciousness of his surroundings, and of all the events that take place within them, is at best 'sleepy'. Because of this condition he is, paradoxically, more deeply affected by what does take place around him; full consciousness would afford him greater protection, an ability to distance himself from the events. The becoming-aware process proceeds gradually until, between the ages of 3 and 5, we could describe the stage of consciousness as having a 'dreaming' quality.

Waldorf early childhood teachers refer to this stage of consciousness as 'dream' consciousness. The realm of dreams embraces the world of symbols, and a young child is able inwardly to transform a stick into a sword, a snake or a horse; a box into a boat, a bed or an oven. (Two boys spent an entire morning in my kindergarten conversing through pieces of wood – their mobile phones!) The child is naturally 'a magician'. The world of matter meets with fantasy and imagination, and is endlessly transformed, becoming symbol. When deeply engaged in play, children are at-one, fully within the activity. They are totally participating in the moment. They are naturally 'writers', re-writing the world anew each day.

Undermining Play and the Ability to Imagine

Arising from this understanding we can see that any situation which accelerates a child's awakefulness consequently diminishes her ability to re-enter the world of imaginative play. 'Awakening' conditions include constant over-stimulation whereby children become too self-conscious, too self-aware to lose themselves in the dream-like condition which is necessary for play. Sadly we see more and more children who are unable to play. Television 'freezes' the child's ability to produce his own 'pictures'; instead, he adopts the images offered by the television's programmes. We have a generation of children wounded by caricature. Early school entry, anxiety-producing inconsistencies in life-styles – all these too-common factors weaken the ability fully to enter into healthy play.

On a more simple and direct level, children at play need to have their privacy respected. Prompting questions and intrusive comments also have a tendency to pull the child out of the condition necessary for this quality of play. (Imagine yourself writing a book, composing a tune, painting a picture – and being constantly interrupted with questions and comments – 'What is it going to be?'; 'Aren't you clever!'; 'Make it a bit bigger…') The Waldorf Kindergarten teacher will support play, but not attempt to 'extend' play in order to impose her own purpose (e.g. to lead a child away from his own personal intention and towards some numerical or literary 'goal') thereby dismantling the very essence of true play and robbing the child of satisfaction when his own 'goal' has been achieved.

As well as sufficient time and suitable space for play, children will need the right equipment to enable them to play out their imagination and fantasy. Equipment which is not 'frozen' but has an open-ended potential best supports the needs of play. A toy fire-engine can only be that; baskets of old bedspreads, a collection

'I' and 'you', *The Lindens Kindergarten, Stroud, England.*

of wooden boxes, a number of planks, baskets of shells and driftwood – these can be re-assembled constantly to become houses today, trains tomorrow, a shop the day after that. They serve the child well. Waldorf kindergartens provide equipment which encourages children to see the potential in situations, and the possible connections between one thing and another. This is a valuable foundation for creative thinking at a later stage.

> *Recently I heard of an ex-Waldorf pupil who, while backpacking in India after leaving school, became concerned by the number of handicapped people he met in rural areas who lacked the financial means to acquire wheelchairs. He responded to the challenge by designing a basic wheelchair structure which could be assembled from materials available from most Indian waste-dumps. He set up workshops to teach the handicapped people how to assemble these wheelchairs themselves from whatever was available in their surroundings.*
>
> *I thought to myself: this is what happens everyday in my kindergarten during creative play: raw materials are used by the children with imagination, visionary zeal and adaptability!*

The human ability 'to imagine' should not be under-valued – it is the source of true genius – and its roots are to be found in the creative play of early childhood. Within the freedom of true play (as opposed to 'structured play') an adaptive intelligence is encouraged.

The Significance of Play for Future Development

Let's return to Barnaby the builder. Clearly he had seen central heating being installed at some time. This activity must have made a deep impression on him, to the extent that he was drawn to re-enact this activity. His play was an act of imitation. It was no mean feat to balance the planks against the bricks, and he demonstrated admirable perseverance and patience as a number fell down and needed to be replaced. He also found that the rope was often not long enough, and he had to go off to find more pieces of rope and tie them together. The use of the rope to represent pipes was an imaginative response to a challenge, and revealed commendable initiative.

Megan's arrival at Elsa's and Paloma's 'house' also presented a challenge. Finding a solution strengthened social skills and revealed the development of 'emotional intelligence' (tolerance, empathy, flexibility, kindness). Negotiation and compromise allowed a healthy flow between what 'I' want and what 'you' need. The transformation of home to hospital, potato to remedy, neighbour to nurse, displayed a flexible, transforming, metamorphic quality within the role play.

The communal construction of the Christmas tree also embraced thinking, problem-solving, co-operation, artistic vision, physical skills. Admirable initiative was called for in making use of what was available, rather than giving up because 'real' greenery was missing. A perfect example of integrated learning.

In all four situations, individual children found opportunity for self-expression and self-direction. These two qualities are always found in creative play, and in turn they strengthen self-confidence and self-esteem. All the children were able to experience 'I can do it!'. This is particularly significant when, on the one hand, we have a society which values self-confidence, and yet at the same time increasingly places children in educational situations where they are over-stretched and experience 'I can't do it!' or 'I'm only just coping'.

Stages of Play

The significant role of play in early childhood development has been well documented, for example by Froebel and Piaget. That the type of play expressed by children evolves in stages has also been widely noted, and personal observation by parents, students and teachers will readily confirm these findings, unless children have been denied the opportunity fully to enter into each phase.

Birth to three years

The earliest form of play activity arises through a combination of sensory experience and motor activity, i.e. sensory-motor based play. A baby will begin to play with his hands or toes, then a rattle, a soft toy. Mother's pots and pans come next, then the sandpit, then onwards and outwards into the wider world with its endless sense impressions and opportunity to respond with movement – touching, tasting, lifting, moving.

Three to five years

In these middle years of childhood we need to note one very important fact – that this is the peak time for imaginative, creative play; and yet, so often, this is the very time when children are being placed into formal schooling environments with their diminished opportunities for creative play. In the school setting, the key environmental criteria for play – sufficient time and appropriate space – are often absent, and the rapid appeal to the 'head' leads to a visible shrivelling up of imaginative expression which is a 'heart and hand' experience.

The young four year old suddenly finds himself surrounded by expectations and imposed purpose. A child's play lacks purpose in this sense, as in adult's work, but purpose is replaced by satisfaction. The child's sense of satisfaction in his play is akin to the adult's sense of purpose in her work. Sadly, adults are increasingly attempting to arouse this adult-like sense of purpose in the pre-school situation, and as a result children are then left to carry an unnecessary and inappropriate burden.

This is the main phase of symbolic-fantasy play. Objects are endowed with the fantasy forces arising naturally within the child – conkers become potatoes, a box a table, water and sand combine to make a chocolate cake. This activity also signals the foundation stage for the development of thinking, a type of thinking 'in pictures'. A child sees a box, and an inner image arises of a boat, and he proceeds to use it as a boat. This early type of 'thinking' needs to be acknowledged and worked with before accelerating children into the next phase of a more awake, intellectual type of thought process. That children can be driven to read and write at four does not necessarily mean that it is a healthy, appropriate – or necessary – activity for them.

Five to seven years

During this time, teachers can detect the beginnings of idea-based play (see Chapter 3). The Waldorf teacher recognizes this important fundamental change as one of the signals that the child is ready for a more cognitive approach to learning. For the four and five year old, learning needs to arise implicitly, from within his own personal, interactive involvement with a situation. He then makes visible 'statements' of his experiences – in his drawings, constructions, role play, the things he says. This is *his* literacy, which we can 'read' if we are only open to it.

But most of all, it calls for our respect; not the signal that it is somehow inferior in relation to the written word. A six year old can now begin to move toward a more explicit learning situation, gradually taking a more independent stance in the learning process.

In the Waldorf kindergarten, every effort will be made to provide conditions in which play can flourish – sufficient time, appropriate space and equipment, but most of all an attitude of respect toward this most magical characteristic of childhood.

'That is why play is so important; it is young children's only defense against the many real or imagined attacks and slights they encounter. In play, children can assert their competence.... Through dramatic play and role-playing, they can assert their competence to assume adult roles eventually. And through their play with peers they assert their social competence, their ability to make and keep friends. Play is always a transformation of reality in the service of the self.

This function of play in early childhood, as a means of reasserting the child's sense of competence is often misunderstood. It is either rationalized as the 'child's work' by which is meant another way in which children learn reading, writing, and science. Or it is explained as the avenue through which children express their creative powers, with the suggestion that they need some formal instruction in expressing themselves more adequately....

The misunderstanding regarding the function of play for young children often results in miseducation. If play is thought of as the child's 'work' then it may be translated into a lesson plan. A child playing store may be asked to put prices on his wares and total up the sales. And if play is thought of as the expression of the child's creative impulse, she may be asked to say what her drawing or painting is and to make the sky and grass more conventional colours. Unfortunately, such treatments of the child's play do not encourage the sense of competence, but rather the reverse; they contribute to a sense of helplessness.'

David Elkind, Miseducation: Preschoolers at Risk

Listening to the 'speech' of the environment

Chapter 7

Sensory Nourishment in Early Childhood

Man has become the sense being which he is, within the physical world, in order to be able to enrich his inner-being through that which he absorbs through the impressions of the physical senses.

Rudolf Steiner, Berlin lecture, 1908

The Right Just To 'Be'

One clear, sunny autumn day I was sweeping up leaves along the kindergarten path. Three-year-old Noah stood watching me for some time. After ten minutes or so he began scooping up leaves with his bare hands and dropping them into the bucket. Occasionally he stopped to inspect a particular leaf with great interest; once or twice he smelled them. A further ten minutes into the activity he discovered a worm. He placed it on the palm of his hand and watched it with devoted attentiveness.

Then he took a few steps toward me and shyly held his hand out to me. I was about to speak when suddenly I knew: nothing needed to be added to this moment between us. It was perfection. Leaf, sun, worm, soil – Noah was listening to the 'speech' of his surroundings, and in the privacy of his uninterrupted 'beingness' he was able to hear.

'I remember being struck by the beauty and order of the room', remarked a new kindergarten parent. The first impression of a

Waldorf kindergarten is often a strongly visual one. Parents frequently refer to the presence of coloured play-cloths, natural fabrics, organic food, wooden floors and furniture, pastel walls, and note the absence of teaching-charts and plastic toys. This description of an aesthetically pleasing environment will most often come before any attempt to explain the aims and activities of the kindergarten. Clearly the sight of the kindergarten room makes an impact upon new parents. This impact makes an even deeper impression upon a young child.

Further observation soon reveals that it isn't just a matter of a visually appealing environment. In using the play-cloths the child *touches* silk and cotton; the wooden toys and furniture *smell* of beeswax; at snack-time she will *taste* the full flavour of unprocessed food, free of chemicals and preservatives; before a puppet show begins she will *hear* the delicate sounds of a lyre or the soft tinkle of a bell or xylophone. Festival celebrations are a veritable feast of touch, smell, sight, taste and sound.

Every day, in many ways, the teacher will be consciously providing 'food' for the senses, keeping the children 'finely tuned' so that in time they will become open and discriminating toward the 'speech' of the environment.

The Child's At-Oneness with the Environment

Rudolf Steiner emphasized the openness of children in the first seven years. He went so far as to describe them as 'wholly sense organ', and their relationship to their surroundings as a type of 'bodily-religious' experience. How does this impressionable openness come about? For the answer, we need to look at two developmental characteristics of the first seven years.

Firstly, our knowledge and understanding of our surroundings is made possible through the senses. They are our gateway to the outer world and the world's inroad to our personal inner space. How does that work? The eye might see a moving form. This is a percept. The sense of sight then conveys this impression, via the nerve-sense system, to the brain, and thought processes begin which allow us to identify the moving form – perhaps as someone we know. This is now a concept.

The senses – in this case, the sense of sight – allow us to encounter a world of percepts, but this is only a part of reality. We need our thinking ability to identify and name our perceptions. Concepts then arise which can remain as memory even after the original percepts have disappeared. This thought-forming, reflective activity makes us conscious beings, and gives us a certain distance from our surroundings, a type of standing back as observer. For the small child this type of conceptual activity isn't yet active, and so she does not experience herself as yet fully separated or 'other' than his surroundings.

Secondly, as we move toward adulthood, we develop an increasing self-identity or ego-consciousness. Accumulated experience and the developing capacity for thinking strengthen this feeling of 'I'. Again, this self-experience isn't yet fully in place for the young child – the boundary between 'I' and surroundings is not experienced so sharply. The child is not fully aware of herself as standing independently, separately, within her environment. She is not yet an 'island' within the world. She still retains the blessed gift of at-oneness. Mind has not yet brought about the discomfort of division.

These two developmental characteristics leave the young child connected, rather than disconnected, from her sensory experiences. She is, as it were, united with sensation, and therefore deeply affected by what it conveys, and her psychological development is influenced by the immediate surroundings. Carl Jung emphasized that the less conscious we are, the greater the impact of experience upon the psyche, and the more potent is that initial impact in determining future behaviour.

This is what Steiner meant by 'wholly sense organ'. The 'bodily-religious' description refers to a type of physical surrendering which operates from the child as she interacts with her environment. She gives herself up to experience with a quality which could be described as devotional. Just watch a child at play! This impressive self-lessness deserves our respect and protection.

(Rudolf Steiner described 12 distinct senses, and a full description of each can be found in the books named in the List of Further Reading at the end of the book.)

'Over the last ten years we have come to know much more about how the brain functions and how experiences are laid down. This new knowledge startlingly demonstrates that our brains are not heavily pre-programmed but they develop largely through experience and that early experiences in particular have a profound influence on how our brains are structured and our minds develop.'

Sir David Winkley, *Current Neurological Research and Its Implications for Educators'*

Developing artistic skills

The nimbleness of weaving and embroidering lays a
foundation for 'nimble' thoughts
Michael Hall Kindergarten, Forest Row, England

The seasons offer opportunities 'to do'
The Lindens Kindergarten, Stroud, England

Becoming creative
The Lindens Kindergarten, Stroud, England

Festivals surround the child in his community – a moment of wonder
and reverence
The Khululeka Education Centre, South Africa

A Father shapes baking dough in the Sophia Project for homeless families
The Sophia Project, San Francisco, USA

"Grandparents, mothers and fathers join a Spring Festival celebration."
Rosebridge May Festival, Cambridge, England

Time to grind the rice, to make the flour – for snacktime!
Panyotai Waldorf Kindergarten, Bangkok, Thailand

Baking birthday cake
Taska Nania, Penang, Malaysia

Making apple juice
Michael Hall Kindergarten, Sussex, England

Hard work for an Easter Festival
Michael Hall Kindergarten, Sussex, England

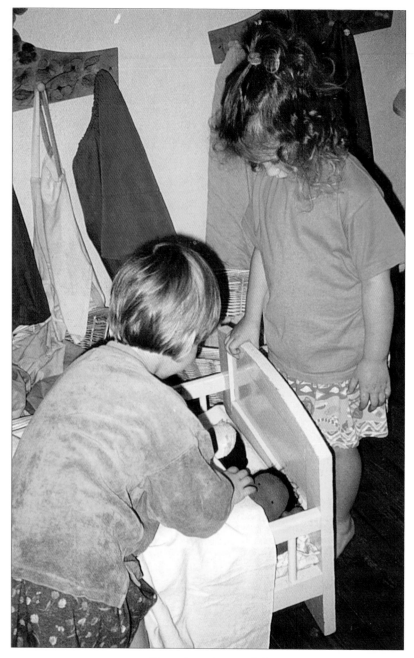

'A gentle caring touch.'
The Lindens Kindergarten, Stroud, England

Let's pretend…
Sloka Waldorf Kindergarten, Hyderabad, India

The World is constantly being transformed
The Lindens Kindergarten, Stroud, England

Preparing the ground for compost. So much to do!
The Lindens Kindergarten, Stroud, England

Time to thresh the rice
Panyotai Waldorf Kindergarten, Bangkok, Thailand

Pumpkin time! Taking pulp for pumpkin pie
Michael Hall Kindergarten, Forest Row, England

Life's work – windows need to be cleaned!
Michael Hall Kindergarten, Forest Row, England

Snacktime provides the opportunity to learn new skills
Taska Nania, Penang, Malaysia

An idea is given a visible expression
The Lindens Kindergarten, Stroud, England

Exploring the language of colour and form through drawing
The Lindens Kindergarten, Stroud, England

Together we can make a new garden
The Lindens Kindergarten, Stroud, England

A Mother and Teacher share a child's birthday celebration
Taska Nania Kindergarten, Penang, Malaysia

Ringtime within a Kindergarten in
a converted bus, South Africa

Nelson Mandela congratulates graduates of a Waldorf Teacher Training
Centre For Creative Education, Cape Town, South Africa

The Impact of Sensory Experience

The senses make their impact physically, cognitively and emotionally. The vulnerable, trusting, developing child is quite literally formed (and informed) by her environment and all that takes place within it. Because of her openness she is educated by sense experience in early childhood. It must therefore be of primary importance to early childhood teachers that the quality of sensory experience is worthy.

Everything that you will encounter in a Waldorf kindergarten is connected in some way to this fundamental thought. The soft pastel walls, the absence of caricature and 'untrue' plastic food and plastic tools; the use of water colours and beeswax crayons; the care of the environment. The 'integrity' and 'quality' of materials and experience is considered to be of prime importance, and their effect upon the child, both immediately and in the long term, is not undervalued.

Sensory Nutrition

We can feel comfortable in using the term 'sensory nutrition' when describing the provision of these quality sense impressions, for this is a form of nourishment, a soul nourishment, as real as the physical nourishment provided by food. 'We are what we eat' might equally be matched with 'The child is what she experiences'.

The brain's development is experience dependent. The direct pathway of the senses, via the central nervous system, to the brain ensures that the physical body is affected by the child's experience. These are 'written into' his body. We can readily observe how our breathing becomes more rapid if we are frightened; how the sight of something unpleasant makes the skin pale. Long-term, future health can reveal the effect, either positively or negatively, of the quality of accumulated experience.

Similarly, experience is internalized and calls up a feeling response – e.g. darkness might arouse anxiety, and returning light bring a feeling of relief. All that children are exposed to provokes an emotional response which can significantly influence their future emotional orientation.

In the first seven years, children are deeply impressed by what we *do*. After this turning point, development will be increasingly guided by what we say. This early non-verbal form of education can be extended to include sight, smell, touch – all that is 'fed' to the child through the senses, in addition to the spoken word.

Protecting Childhood

For some years now, Waldorf educators have been considering the question, 'Do we need to develop, quite consciously, an education of the senses?' – or further still, a *therapy* for the senses? Increasingly, the early childhood curriculum concerns itself with an intellectual education, and the resulting imbalance in terms of impoverished sensory encounter is in need of redress.

The world and the individual spirit meet at the doorway of the senses; the world enters, makes its mark, and then we go out to re-create the world anew, according to these influences. *What images and influences do we wish to 'feed' to the spirit of the young child?*

The Loss of Innocence

'...up until they [children] are six or seven years old they are developmentally, psychologically, physically unable to discern the difference between fantasy and reality.

This means that when a young child sees somebody on TV being shot, stabbed, raped, brutalized, degraded, or murdered, to them it is as though it were actually happening. In the end some of them embrace violence and accept it as a normal and essential survival skill in a brutal new world.

On June 10, 1992, the Journal of the American Medical Association (JAMA*) published a definitive epidemiological study on the impact of TV violence. In nations, regions, or cities where television appears there is an immediate explosion of violence on the playground, and within 15 years there is a doubling of the murder rate. Why 15 years? That's how long it takes for a brutalized two year old to reach the "prime crime" years. That's how long it takes before you begin to reap what you sow when you traumatize and desensitize a toddler or a five year old.*

The JAMA concluded that "the introduction of television in the 1950s caused a subsequent doubling of the homicide rate, i.e. long term childhood exposure to television is a causal factor behind approximately one-half of the homicides committed in the United States, or approximately 10,000 homicides annually".'

Extract from Lt. Col. Dave Grossman, 'Teaching kids to kill', in The Future of Childhood *(Hawthorn Press)*

Adults, parents, grandparents and teachers, working together, can act as guardians for our children, standing on the threshold between world and child, lovingly responsible until a time when the child, undamaged as a result of this early protective gesture, can take personal responsibility for what she allows to influence her.

Often parents ask, 'Are Waldorf educators *too* protective? Shouldn't we be preparing the child for the *real* world?'. It is debatable as to just what is 'real' in this sense. Are we offering children a 'virtual reality', a second-hand 'almost' reality, rather than the integrity of a true, direct, perception of the world in which they live?

'It is ironic that many observers of the Waldorf kindergarten... initially perceive it as a "sheltered" situation. To a degree, this is true: during the school day, Waldorf kindergarteners are protected from the media, electronic devices, synthetic noises and processed foods. On the other hand, unlike most urban and suburban preschoolers, Waldorf kindergarteners are exposed to a great deal as well; the realities of food preparation, the wind, the rain, warmth and cold, and brambles and briars (on their daily walks). In some settings they encounter sheep and goats, birds and fish "in the raw", uncaged, unlabeled and even unplugged. (Encountering animals that are unaccompanied by explanatory labels or animated software may not be "educational" but such meetings are quite memorable and very real.) So which child is the "sheltered" one, and which is the child really meeting life?'

Eugene Schwartz, Millennial Child

Sensory Overload - the More, More, More Generation

Fool's Gold...

For the majority [of children], computers pose health hazards and potentially serious developmental problems... 'Must five-years-olds be trained on computers today to get the high-paying jobs of tomorrow? *The technology in schools today will be obsolete long before five-year-olds graduate. Creativity and imagination are prerequisites for innovative thinking, which will never be obsolete in the workplace. Yet a heavy diet of ready-made computer images and programmed toys appears to stunt imaginative thinking. Teachers report that children in our electronic society are becoming alarmingly deficient in generating their own images and ideas.*

Do computers really "connect" children to the world? *Too often, what computers actually connect children to are trivial games, inappropriate adult material, and aggressive advertising. They can also isolate children, emotionally and physically, from direct experience of the natural world. The "distance" education they promote is the opposite of what all children, and especially children at risk, need most – close relationships with caring adults.'*

Extracted from: Fool's Gold: A Critical Look at Computers in Childhood *(Alliance for Childhood, College Park, MD, 2000)*

It is clearly most important, then, that we consider the quality of sensory encounter; but increasingly we now also need to look at the *quantity* of sensations children receive in their daily lives. 'Quality time' is now being superseded by 'thrill time', a journalist recently noted when reflecting upon the frenzied, insatiable reactions of a group of young children to a birthday party where every effort had been made to provide a variety of stimulating activities, but 'What are we going to do *now?*' still rang out as the persistent response.

Many teachers are observing sensory fatigue in children, a type of shut-down which, when matched with physical fatigue from their hectic schedules, means that children are quite literally falling asleep in kindergartens. Sensory deprivation can, of course, have catastrophic results. Children in institutions, neglected children, reveal to us the painful effect of being denied healthy sensory stimulation. It is now a bitter irony that children in 'civilized', materially rich societies are demonstrating the effect of the opposite pole – *sensory overload*. The child's excitability finds a naturally, soothing antidote in the Waldorf Kindergarten environment.

The Effects of Television on Young Children's Developing Brain and Senses

The epidemic of symptoms stemming from our culture's increasingly (ubiquitous television and computer) – for example, repetitive strain injury, eye strain, childhood obesity and so-called 'attention deficit disorder' – leads one to question the wisdom of young children's excessive exposure to these electronic media. Over 70 per cent of British children now have a television, video and computer in their bedroom, and, even more disturbingly, a quarter of under-fours in Britain have their own television set. So just what is the evidence regarding the effects of these media on the brain and the senses?

According to neurological researcher Dr Jane M. Healy, television viewing affects both the growing brain and learning abilities, such

---

as the capacity to sustain attention, listen attentively, read with understanding and hold conversations. Television can overstimulate children, causing passive withdrawal – the 'zombie look'. Moreover, the television's fast pace and special effects reduce the capacity for vigilance, and the brain 'tunes out' in response to television exposure, indicating more passive alpha brain patterns.

Healy maintains that television and related media may well: (1) reduce the stimulation of left brain systems critical for language development, reading and analytical thinking; (2) affect mental ability and attention by decreasing interchange between the brain's hemispheres; and (3) undermine the development of the executive systems that control attention, organization and motivation. She considers that, based on the extant research, young, developing brains are just not ready for the television media – not least because a normal sensory 'diet' pattern is considered necessary to stimulate the brain's healthy development.

Thus, the sense of sight and movement are both needed to 'see', and constant eye movement is needed for healthy eyes – yet television stills the eyes into a fixed stare. The cramping of movement so commonly associated with regular TV viewing can have disruptive effects such as hyperactivity, impulsive behaviour, and a kind of 'motor sickness' which causes letters to move up and down the visual field. Moreover, for the development of healthy social skills and language, children need to play and to converse with real people, so they can grasp a sense for language, and a feel for the reality of relationships with other people.

Overall, the electronic media offer a very poor sensory diet; and the disturbing message from neurological research like that of Jane Healy is that the electronic media can undermine brain development – and that play, everyday family life, a calm,

> *television-free environment and creative activities are far better for children's growing brain and senses.*
>
> Reference*: Jane M. Healy, Ph.D.,* Endangered Minds: Why Children Can't Think and What We Can Do About It *(Simon and Schuster, New York, 1991)*
>
> **Martin Large,**
> **Who's Bringing Them Up? How to Kick the T.V. Habit**
> *(Hawthorn Press, Stroud, 1992)*

Emotional Indifference

The experience-dependent nature of the brain means that the brain organization is always, however slowly, adapting. Where is it going? In the 1980s, bio-psychological research at the University of Tuebingen in Germany revealed that the senses of smell, taste, sight and hearing were requiring a higher level of stimulation before the brain would register a response – i.e. the experiences needed to be smellier, saltier, sweeter, louder!

Henner Ertel, a psychologist from Munich, stated: 'The receptivity of the senses of smell and taste had degenerated significantly.... The brain had set a new sensation threshold and had refused to recognize sensations that were below this new limit, sensations that would have been unconditionally accepted before. The brain refused to take action on a significant proportion of the stimuli. It was getting more and more difficult to stimulate the corresponding centres in the cerebral cortex.' In other words, the brain was calling for more, more, more.

This response threshold also has worrying moral implications. As we are increasingly exposed to images of murder, death and brutality on our television sets, at the cinema and in our video games, an *emotional indifference* begins to reveal itself. Images which, 50 years ago, would not have been seen by children, and would have provoked revulsion even in the adult viewer, are now observed with apparent indifference. Instead of sensitivity, we are witnessing a worrying de-sensitization. The quality of sensory experience in early childhood can make a major contribution to the 'humanizing' process so valued by Waldorf educators.

Children themselves have become murderers, as we have witnessed in a series of disturbing incidents throughout the world. On a less extreme level, but equally deserving of our concern, childhood ill-health is increasing in areas like asthma, allergic reactions, eczema and hyperactivity. The polluted landscape of childhood is as much in need of our attention as are environmental issues.

Protecting the Child's Imaginative Potential

'Failing to develop imagery means having no imagination. This is far more serious than not being able to daydream. It means children who can't "see" what the mathematical symbol or the semantic words mean; nor what the chemical formulae, nor the concept of civilization as we know it [mean].

They can't comprehend the subtleties of our Constitution or Bill of Rights and are seriously (and rightly) bored by abstractions of this sort. They can sense only what is immediately bombarding their physical system and are restless and ill-at-ease without such bombardment. Being sensory deprived they initiate stimulus through constant movement or intensely verbal interaction with each other, which is often mistaken for precocity but is actually a verbal hyperactivity filling the gaps of the habituated bombardments.'

Joseph Chilton Pearce, Evolution's End

Children sometimes need the quiet, patient attentiveness of adults

Chapter 8

When Are Children Ready for School?

*It is absolutely essential that before we begin to think, before
we so much as begin to set our thinking in motion, we experience
the condition of wonder.*

Rudolf Steiner, 'The world of the senses and the world of the spirit'

'The Hurried Child'

Nowhere is the disturbing phenomenon of 'the hurried child'
more visible than in the pressure to submit children to a formal
learning experience at an increasingly younger age. The entire
mood of a Waldorf kindergarten arises from the intention to
awaken and preserve a sense of wonder in the young child. The
relationship to nature, the rich imagery of fairy-tales, the
magical quality of puppetry, the awe and reverence experienced
in the celebration of festivals, the mood and 'inner gesture' of
the teachers themselves – the child enters an environment where
wonder is acknowledged as the foundation for the development
of a natural seeker of knowledge. Wonder is the very seed of
enquiry.

In creative, imaginative play the child has discovered the wisdom
of 'Seek and ye shall find'; play constantly offers opportunity for
self-initiated discovery and the child's own personal efforts to
seek solutions to the problems he meets in the process. He has
developed the habit of being an active participant in the learning
experience.

During the time in the kindergarten the children will meet many natural, unforced opportunities for taking the first steps toward the development of numeracy skills. Finger rhymes, the sorting of play objects into baskets at clearing time, the setting of the table, the counting of chairs for story-time. Always in a meaningful context and without a premature appeal to consciousness.

The six year olds are notably articulate as they have met a rich language content in the stories, the many songs and verses of ring-time (often in a foreign language), and have extended their own vocabulary as a result of the repetitive element in the presentation of these opportunities. In addition, they have the most important prerequisites for literacy – sound listening and attention skills. Whilst the Waldorf kindergarten is not a book-filled environment, it is most definitely a word-rich experience. The time and space provided for free play has ensured that these early pre-literacy skills have been exercised and strengthened as the children interact with other children, and speech is stimulated in the process of role-play.

A Word-rich Experience as a Foundation for Literacy

'Every person or group of persons who move into literacy first build a foundation for reading and writing in the world of orality. Orality supports literacy, provides the impetus for shaping it. The skills one learns in orality are crucial because literacy is more than a series of words on paper. It is a set of relationships and structures, a dynamic system that one internalizes and maps back onto experience. A person's success in orality determines whether he or she will "take" to literacy.... But the way has been blocked. It has been blocked by electronic

---

machinery of every conceivable kind, from TV and movies, through records and CDs, to PCs and video games. Before teachers and parents begin to think about raising literate children, they must first ensure their beings as creatures of orality.'

Barry Sanders, A Is for Ox: Violence, Electronic Media, and the Silencing of the Written Word

A Sense of 'When'

Educationalists – both teachers and policy-makers – and parents are in danger of losing a sense of the progressive nature of child development, a sense of *when*, and the importance of choosing both a curriculum and a means of delivering the curriculum which will acknowledge and enhance each stage of development. In this way our children are unhurried and protected from undue anxiety and unnecessary expectations which can so often result in behavioural difficulties or a feeling of inadequacy. Then comes the further burden of being 'labelled' at an early age – difficult, slow learner, social misfit... at five!

After Play – the Next Step

The same principle of 'wholeness' which informs Waldorf education generally also influences the decision about when a child is ready to leave the Waldorf kindergarten and take the giant step toward a more formal, directed, whole-class approach to learning in the middle school years. This entirely different situation demands a very different response from children, and we need to be sure that they have developed the necessary *qualities* to meet the new situation.

We are looking for signs of 'whole-readiness', a readiness in a number of areas of the child's development, not simply a 'cut-off' age-related date for school entry. We also want to feel confident that the child will *flourish* in the next step rather than merely 'coping'.

Timing the Transition

Children will normally make the transition to a Waldorf Class 1 after the sixth birthday. The 'cut-off' date for entry varies somewhat from school to school, though most Waldorf schools will question the readiness of children whose birthdays fall in the three months immediately prior to entry – the summer birthday children. Research has shown that these children, almost a year younger than the oldest children in the class, will frequently struggle to keep up throughout the middle school years. Sometimes they can appear to be doing quite well but then the struggle emerges in the long term, when the demands of puberty find them without the necessary maturational resources to cope with peer pressure, sexuality, the demands of examinations. Boys in particular display the negative effects of being forced too soon into a formal learning situation which requires them to 'be still' and become receivers rather than active participants in the learning situation.

In many countries the instinct for school readiness is still intact: the transition to school is made after the sixth birthday, and the Waldorf schools' entry policy fits in quite comfortably with mainstream policies. However, in other countries (for example, in England), the legal age for entry has been lowered to the fifth birthday, and in recent years considerable encouragement has been given to parents to send children as young as four. The fact that each school receives funding per child means that the decision to bring the child into the school environment is not always one made in the best interest of the individual child's needs. The date of birth becomes the only criterion for such an important decision which could affect the child's well-being well into the future.

After Entry – What Then?

The next pertinent issue is what, precisely, the children then *experience*, at such a tender age, in the next setting. Unfortunately, the educational climate is often such that the formal teaching of numeracy, literacy and the introduction to information technology immediately begins. Parents are also vulnerable to any atmosphere of competitiveness that might prevail, and are naturally anxious to be reassured that their child will not be disadvantaged in the 'race' that then begins. Playtime and play-space are withdrawn and children can be required to surrender their love of movement to the expectation of 'being still', 'paying attention', memorizing and achievement in assessment procedures. There is a premature 'contraction of [the child's] world of possibilities, a cramping of [the child's] creative potential' (Eugene Schwartz, 'Millennial Child')

Education as a Journey – Not a Race

The sixth birthday is seen as a turning-point by many educationalists: certain things are possible after this milestone that are not possible before – or, at least, should not be *forced* from the child before the sixth birthday. The fact that children *can* achieve numeracy and literacy skills is often seen as providing justification for such intervention. The question could be re-phrased: *what is lost in the process, and what are the **long-term** consequences of such precocious achievements?*

In order to benefit and to perform in memorizing and conceptual activity, without a weakening of overall well-being, a pre-school child needs to have established a firm foundation on to which the new skills can be built. Certain phases of development need to have been completed, and certain qualities and capacities need to have emerged. The child needs to be 'ready' on a number of levels in his development, not only ready cognitively, but physically, socially and emotionally.

A birth date is insufficient evidence of readiness for the demands which will be made upon him once he enters the school environment. The price paid for such 'acceleration' can have its effects well into adulthood, and any feelings of having under-performed can haunt us long into the future.

The Problem of Movement

Increasing media reports of teachers' frustrations with children's disruptive behaviour (dropping pencils, getting off chairs, calling out at inappropriate times, not 'sitting still', not 'paying attention') may indicate that many children are entering the first year of school unready to stop movement for the periods of time required to attain the desired numeracy and literacy skills. In Waldorf education there is a fundamental principle that when determining the time for a transition from kindergarten to school, the child should have completed the phase of development whereby she learns almost entirely through doing. Only then will she *willingly* offer her co-operation – as opposed to being coerced – in a more formal learning situation. This quality will not be evident until the play-based learning phase from the third to fifth year has run its course.

Attempting to cut short this phase will result in a 'damming up' of the need to explore the world through movement, and the resulting frustration in some children can only result in 'explosions' of movement. We need to look for signs that the child is ready to overcome the need to move – to self-control and self-direct – rather than movement needing to be forced into stillness.

In the final year of the Waldorf kindergarten, as the children turn six, we will see signs of the need to move being overshadowed by the need to give expression to ideas. Six year olds will take delight in, and even request, a variety of activities (handwork, woodwork, drawing, modelling, weaving, sewing) which require a longer span of attentiveness and perseverance. They will take a real pleasure in their own skills and in the completion of the activity. They spend less time in creative play, preferring to sit by a teacher and learn from the teacher's skills. They are noticeably more confident, responsible and independent. The transition from the chaotic movement at two to the directed, purposeful mood of the six year olds reveals a new ability willingly to be 'attentive', an important foundation for the commencement of formal learning.

Movement for movement's sake, as an expression of energy, has become movement for *an idea's* sake, which is just what numeracy and literacy is all about. *Now* the class teacher can begin his work without undue obstacles. The pre-school teacher can bring this great gift – children who are truly, fully ready; and the work of the school teacher is then far more efficient as a consequence.

A Positive Attitude toward Movement

Do we, as adults, view children's movement as an inconvenience?… even to the extent that we will 'numb' increasing numbers of children with the drug Ritalin, in order to stop their activity? (In October 2000, a British BBC Radio 4 programme quoted statistics which included 150,000 children in the UK on Ritalin, and as many as *1 in 5 children* in the USA on the same drug.) Of course, there are children who are truly in need of medical help for severe behavioural disturbances, but the scale and acceleration of prescribed drug-taking in children – some as young as three – should sound alarm bells for concerned adults.

Perhaps children's movement on this scale is only a problem in relation to adult expectation. If we expect them to 'be still' and they aren't – then it is clearly a problem. If we don't expect them to cease moving – if, in fact, we acknowledge it as a necessity and welcome it, work *with it*, rather than against it, then the problem disappears! Having 'run its course' and come under the child's own control in ways described in the previous chapters of this book, then the child is *ready*, in this aspect of her development, to move forward into the next stage of a more teacher-directed phase of education. The child can be observed to have made the transition from habitual imitation to the ability to accept instruction without obvious signs of frustration.

Emotional Readiness

The concept of 'multiple intelligence' is gaining ground. Daniel Goleman's popular book *Emotional Intelligence* challenged our preoccupation with 'brain-bound' thinking. The widening of our concept of 'intelligence' can lead us to consider *emotional* readiness for school entry. This would embrace the child's interaction with other children; response to problems and obstacles he may meet; ability to work in a group (and not always need to have his own way!); a willingness to accept what needs to be done, rather than what *he* wants to be done; equally, not to always be submissive to the demands of other children – and many qualities which reveal themselves in the emotional aspect of his development.

If a child enters school before he is fully ready in the emotional developmental dimension, then important social skills will be missing; and under the pressure to perform academically, and within the restrictions of a more controlled situation, this can lead to inappropriate behaviour in the long run.

It is only in the final year of the kindergarten that the children begin to reveal wonderful and desirable social skills – caring for the younger children, offering support and willing co-operation to the teacher, becoming conscious of appropriate behaviour – and they take these valuable skills into the next step of their education.

The Necessary Stamina for the School Experience

Classes are often large in comparison to the group size in pre-school situations. Classes of 30 with one teacher (perhaps with an assistant) are not uncommon. In the pre-school setting the child receives more individual attention and is less pressurized to 'keep up'. In the school playground (frequently cramped, and with hard surfaces that cannot yield many possibilities for play), the young four or five year old has to enter larger, boisterous, even frightening groups of children, often with inadequate adult supervision. The school day is longer, and very rapidly the parents feel the pressure to send their child full time: the demands are greater, and children soon begin to show signs of physical and emotional exhaustion. Physical readiness is missing.

By delaying school entry until after the sixth birthday, we can ensure that children have the necessary stamina to meet what will be required of them. With asthma, hyperactivity, eczema and stress-related illnesses on the increase in young children, the question of stamina needs our concerned attention. Where children are making the transition from a Waldorf kindergarten into mainstream education, parents can resist any pressure to send the child before the statutory age of entry, confident that an extra year in the kindergarten will literally give the child that bit extra – cognitively, physically and emotionally – to enter the school gate with real strength.

The Changing Relationship to the Teacher

In the final year of the kindergarten, the six year olds can demonstrate a particularly loving and respectful relationship to the teacher if the previous phases have been handled skilfully. They will regularly express a desire to sit by the teacher, stand next to her at ring-time; the girls will give spontaneous 'hugs' and the boys will ask for the teacher's support with their activities. The teacher has, from the child's point of view, made the transition from being an example to imitate to becoming a naturally and lovingly accepted leader. Here is another level of 'readiness' – the readiness to accept knowledge from an authority, whereas previously he learnt by imitating the adult's activity. The child is revealing his readiness to accept the class teacher.

Assessment of School Readiness

In a Waldorf context, chronological factors will, of course, be taken into account because at some point clearly the child *has* to enter the school environment, and cut-off dates, for many practical reasons, do have to be established. However, there will always be space given to the unique needs of each child – for the individual child remains the most important factor in the decision-making process. Certain guidelines have been developed by Waldorf teachers, arising from their experience, observation of children and insights gained from the principles of Waldorf education. These guidelines form the basis of conversations between a number of interested and involved individuals whose prime concern is the child's well-being, both immediately and long term. Parents, teachers, the Class 1 teacher and the school doctors can all be part of this conversation. The decisional criteria will be an overall readiness and the unique needs of the individual child.

Once a decision has been reached, the next step is to consider the transition to Class 1. Each kindergarten and school will have its own procedure, but a shared intention is that all the valuable insight gained by the kindergarten teacher during the child's time in the kindergarten should be shared with the new class teacher. A meeting will be arranged with the teacher concerned to share this information (which is considerable over a three-year period). A morning might be spent in the kindergarten observing the group of children who will go up the following year; and some form of 'festival' will frequently be created to mark the handing over of the children from the kindergarten group leader to the Class 1 teacher. Whatever form this sharing takes, what is important is that a 'bridge' is formed from one situation to the next, and that the child is eased into the next experience.

The Hurried Teacher – the Gift of Time

The 'hurried child' is a reflection of the 'hurried teacher'. The increasing pressure to speed children through childhood, the emphasis on results and an atmosphere of competitiveness between child and child, teacher and teacher, school and school; the shrinking of a broad, healthy, curriculum which embraces ideals as much as ideas, down to a narrow 'diet' of numeracy, literacy and information technology; the burdens of paperwork, bureaucracy and accountability – these pressures result in teachers who often seem too stressed to remember their original motivation for entering the teaching profession.

The *qualities* we have been describing in this book – qualities such as enthusiasm, initiative, social skills, emotional and physical stamina, the natural curiosity for learning which is born from the wonder experienced in play, the whole quality of readiness for the next stage of the learning process – these important qualities need time to emerge and to be consolidated. Teachers need time to bring them to fruition, for these are qualities which are as important and as crucial to our well-being as a community as is the child's need to be literate. We need 'literacy' in *all* aspects of our being, and teachers, given the time, can make a valuable contribution to ensuring this on our behalf.

'I remember one morning when I discovered a cocoon in the bark of a tree, just as a butterfly was making a hole in its case and preparing to come out. I waited a while, but it was too long appearing and I was impatient. I bent over it and breathed on it to warm it. I warmed it as quickly as I could and the miracle began to happen before my eyes, faster than life.

The case opened, the butterfly started slowly crawling out, and I shall never forget my horror when I saw how its wings were folded and crumpled; the wretched butterfly tried with its whole trembling body to unfold them. Bending over it , I tried to help it with my breath. In vain. It needed to be hatched out patiently, and the unfolding of the wings should be a gradual process in the sun. Now it was too late. My breath had forced the butterfly to appear, all crumpled before its time. It struggled and, a few seconds later, died on the palm of my hand.

That little body, I do believe, the greatest weight I have on my conscience. For I realise today that it is a mortal sin to violate the great laws of nature. We should not hurry, we should not be impatient, but we should confidently obey the eternal rhythm.'

Nikos Kazantzakis, *Report to Greco*

PART III

CURRENT GLOBAL PRACTICE AND ITS EARLY ROOTS

Children meet a warm welcome in a kindergarten created with courage in difficult circumstances.

The Masince Educare Centre, South Africa

Chapter 9

One River, Many Streams:
Some International Studies

The antidote for power-hunger, hate, sectarianism and
fundamentalism is a loving approach to the other, an
understanding of his difference, sympathy for his capacity to
learn and develop, thanks for his individual spiritual essence.

Ute Craemar, *Favela Children*

In this chapter I present just a few descriptions of Waldorf early childhood activities from around the world. These 'local studies' will give the reader a flavour of the rich multi-cultural diversity of the world-wide Waldorf movement, and they collectively demonstrate that Steiner Waldorf education is quite unique in its internationalism, adaptability and cultural pluralism.

South Africa

The areas surrounding Cape Town are filled with people who have moved to the city in search of work. They live in shacks of corrugated iron, timber and fittings salvaged from building and demolition sites. Essential services such as sanitation and running water are often lacking, and the cycle of poverty and deprivation is difficult to break. Questions of self-esteem and hope become paramount. Courageous and enterprising women have started day-care centres in their homes, sometimes adding wood and iron extensions to their shacks to accommodate the children, occasionally managing to find land or separate buildings.

Waldorf teachers have developed courses to give training and support to these township women. The Centre for Creative Education, Cape Town, places equal emphasis upon the development of practical teaching skills and training experiences which will develop self-belief. Our course participants have had their belief in themselves, their abilities, and their culture eroded by their social circumstances and our apartheid history.

We have to work to allow the suppressed and hidden creative person to emerge and be acknowledged. Self-development is enhanced through eurythmy, painting, drawing, modelling and handwork. A new belief in themselves and their own abilities is the first step towards change. A newly confident care-giver imbues the children with her own positivity and pride in self, people and culture. As the activities and the room change and the simple, beautiful surroundings and playthings are given to the children, it gives them a frame of reference to aspire to, and the foundation skills to achieve it.

(The above extract from 'Partnering Kindergartens in South Africa' Newsletter *is reprinted with the permission of The Centre for Creative Education, South Africa*)

The interaction between the Waldorf trainers and the students from the townships gives a practical foundation to integration and inter-culturalism. The students gradually awaken to a new concept – that children need more than basic shelter and food. The trainers encourage them to collect natural, available materials for their classrooms, to develop the skills (handwork, woodwork, painting) to create their own equipment, and to develop an understanding of the healing nature of play, domestic activities, stories, songs and rhythm – all with a strong reference to their Xhosa culture.

After graduation, the students continue to work in their appropriately named Educare Centres. These centres begin in a backyard, without furniture or toys. They often act as a magnet for parents and children, and a group of 40-50 children is not uncommon.

In 1998 further support was initiated, with the provision of basic play kits for students and Xhosa-speaking fieldworkers to visit the Educare Centres. A 'Partnering Kindergartens in South Africa' scheme has begun, aimed at forming partnerships between Waldorf kindergartens worldwide and these newly emerging South African Waldorf Kindergartens. It is hoped that this inter-cultural, co-operative venture will provide funds, equipment and encouragement. Distance training has begun in Nairobi, Kenya, with Kenyan, Ugandan and Tanzanian students and demonstration centres have been established where students can witness Waldorf education in practice in settings that relate more closely to their own circumstances.

For more information, or to offer support, contact: Center for Creative Education, PO Box 280, Plumstead, Cape Town, South Africa

Brazil

In the late 1970s Ute Craemar, a German teacher working in the Sao Paulo Waldorf School, opened 'escolinha' (the little school) in a favela (slum) named Monte Azul. In 1966

Ute had begun working as a social worker in a favela in Londrina. After completing a Waldorf teacher training in Germany, she returned to a post at the Sao Paulo Waldorf School, as a class teacher. The stark contrast between the lives of her Waldorf students and the conditions endured by small children in the favelas, the home of the poorest of the poor, awakened her awareness of the gulf between the affluent white and destitute black people of Brazil.

Whilst continuing to work as a teacher, Ute maintained her link with the people of the favela and, gradually, a group of 12 young people from the favela came to live with her in Sao Paulo, where she supported their emotional and practical needs. This adopted 'family' in turn attracted further children from the local favela, Monte Azul, who initially came begging for food. She described them as 'children without childhood'. Again, observing the contrast between the children of the Waldorf school who had many opportunities available to them, and the favela children who had so little, Ute had the inspired idea that the Waldorf students should offer something to the children of the favela! *'One morning somewhat timidly I proposed to them my idea for my escolinha for favela children. A rush of enthusiasm. They all had ideas: I can teach the children gymnastics, knitting, handicrafts, and I can play with them. We will collect clothing, crayons, drawing paper. Yes, and where will all this take place? In my house. We can use the old shed in the yard. So it began!' (Ute Craemer in her book* Favela Children)

In her book Ute describes how she would take sometimes as many as 40 favela children to the Waldorf school for performances of the Christmas plays. Trips to the mountains and to the seaside were organized, but the overriding need became clear – more space was required. Ute began collecting discarded building materials, and eventually a plot of land and a financial donation from Germany enabled her to build a plain dwelling on barren land. Today this initial impulse has found its full expression in the Monte Azul Community Association. Ute's original individual efforts are now supported by some 145 permanent collaborators, 60 per cent of whom are favela residents who have been joined by Brazilian and foreign volunteers.

The work has been extended to other favelas, and the methodology of Waldorf education and the insights offered by Anthroposophy have stimulated the following activity: pre-school education for some 400 children, youth centres, workshops offering practical training in carpentry, baking, electrical skills, artistic activities, furniture recycling and kindergarten training, health services, therapeutic practices, and a vibrant cultural programme which attracts performances by Brazilian and international artists. The Association (ACOMA) has attracted awards from Brazilian and international governments.

Ute quotes certain statistics for Brazil – 7 million children living on the streets, half a million in state orphanages, 35 per cent of the population without schooling. The 'escolinha' was a first step toward overcoming a feeling of helplessness when confronted with such a situation. Exploring possible solutions such as changes to the socio-economic system and voluntary aid, she offers her own personal insight on 'Favela Children': *'...improvements will only have a lasting effect if they go hand in hand with a profound understanding of the miracle of man. Knowing the human being not only in his visible, physical form, but also in his original spiritual essence, to recognize in every individual a creative, spiritual self, who has come to earth in order to evolve towards freedom and love and to carry this result into future lives on earth, is an enhanced point of departure for today's social work, social art, social science.*

Once this conviction has impregnated our human encounters, the struggle for each individual soul can develop into a multiplying movement which is a formidable opposition to the forces that are based on hunger for power, self-destructing influences and contempt for humanity.'

(For further information contact Monte Azul Communitarian Association, Av. Tomas de Souza, 552, 05836-350 Sao Paulo, Brazil. Web site: http;//www.sab.org/monteazul/english.htm)

Palestine

In the Gaza strip, Shati is one of the 'worst' and politically 'hottest' of Palestinian refugee camps. Working with the children in it, one needs to be highly awake and flexible. The few hours we spend with the children and adults are usually a time achieved with difficulty: the situation there is constantly changing, the people are living in constant psychological unrest and tension – hence we often have to improvise the time and location of our meetings.

A few examples: my car, usually packed to the roof, more than half-concealing the Israeli and/or Arab friends coming to assist, leaves at 6.30 a.m. in the morning after I have taken pains to collect all the necessary information concerning our destination; yet two hours later we might learn that 'our' camp is on curfew. Or: our driver, who wants to receive us on the other side of the border, has been arrested. Or: 10 minutes after having started sewing and knitting puppets, we are urgently asked to leave the camp because of approaching soldiers, who have the right to enter every house by day and by night (As a German-Israeli I am in no real danger: my sense of fear and tension is caused by my emotional identification with those who are!)

Once, I arrived in the camp with a well-planned programme – to tell fairy-tales and show finger games. But what I did that day was anything but telling stories and finger games: visiting families in need and people in hospital was more urgent. Why do I tell you this? Not because of us, but because of the predicament of the children who go through all this. Every house has its changes and drastic surprises. Going into hiding, running away, arrest of mother and/or father, or other family members – or much worse, bereavement after a fatal shooting.

Constant noises like radio news or music, gun shot, excited conversation, shouting and screaming out of anger, fear, nervousness, demonstrations, clashes, stone-throwing against doors and metal roofs during demonstrations, the crushing noise of a house being torn down, crying and lamenting during a funeral procession. All these are experiences that the Palestinian child of Gaza is living through day after day. And then: anxiety by night-time, sleeplessness - because arrest and expulsion happen usually around 3.30 in the morning, painful memories caused by the unbearable tensions often of the past day, on the streets, in the market, in the kindergarten, at home....

Because of ever-present fear and danger, the child does not know a quiet walk, a peaceful guarding of sheep or goats, fishing, or playing with shells on the shore. The consequences are sleeplessness, bed-wetting, severe health problems like kidney and heart diseases (three year old children!), emotional numbness – and, of course, violence. Little wonder that the games most commonly played are the imitation of beating, throwing stones, arresting, going to prison, shooting and killing.

What I try – though often with a sense of failure and not doing enough – is to calm the children, to bring relief through laughter, a real child's laughter. Even when we sit together and work, one sometimes tends to forget what is happening outside. During my last visit to the camp I built a little shadow-theatre for the 70 children, showing them the old, universal fairy-tale of the 'Starchild' with its ever-repeated images of a human being gently touching another human being. The quiet in the room was heart moving for all.

Recently I met an Arab student who will come with me and help translate: I also met an Arab physician who will accompany me on future visits and serve the children's medical needs. The next plan will be that we will translate stories and finger games into Arabic, and maybe print them for general use in kindergartens in the occupied territories.

During the Summer holidays I also organized some kind of 'workshops' for bigger children, who would otherwise hang around the dangerous streets of the camp – weaving, modelling and painting with them. During the last months before the Iraqi war broke out, the teachers of the camp organized, with my help, a Waldorf bazaar with toys, puppets which we had made together (they continue on their own during curfew times). Such an event is quite endangering – as is any independent activity, political or otherwise. During the last weeks before the war I had to veil myself. In the mean time, the popularity of 'Waldorf' puppetry has spread into many other refugee camps. I sometimes feel that I am working against time; but then again, when I leave the camp I carry the hope that we can suspend, just for a short time, the ever-growing disaster.

(This article describes the time Christiana Levy spent in the refugee camps and previously appeared in Child and Man, *Vol. 25, No.2, and is reproduced here with the permission of the editorial group.)*

North America

The Sophia Project in San Francisco is a model for inner-city childcare. Operating within the early childhood programme at the Raphael House homeless shelter, it was initiated by Carol Cole, the Children's Programme Director. Carol's own work directory includes Montessori, special needs and Waldorf teacher training, followed by practical experience with refugee children and the founding of a multi-cultural kindergarten within a Camphill community in South Africa.

The Sophia Project will develop a centre where mothers and children who are homeless, or at risk of homelessness, can be supported in their endeavours to improve their social situation. Here the image of the human being will be held in its wholeness by all those who will live and work here. The ideal of wholeness will help create an environment in which mothers and children can heal. Through the healing quality of Waldorf education, mothers and children can learn to create healthy, nourishing relationships with each other, the world about them, and, last but not least, with themselves.

There is a need for a community committed to this task; and by experiencing the staff caring collaboratively for the children, the mothers have begun to see the richness that could be brought to their lives through co-operation and trust. The Sophia Centre will create a safe environment for the mothers and children to deepen the experience of trust and co-operation. Aided by such experiences and their work at the centre, they will be able to discover the richness of their own relationships to the world and the fullness of their own being.

We will begin work with one house in a low income neighbourhood in Oakland. The house will hold live-in co-workers, a kindergarten and daycare, with a daycare training classroom for mothers. We hope to expand to three groups of 12 children, serving 36 families in this under-served population. There will be three areas of activity. *First*, work with children – a childcare centre based on Waldorf principles for pre-school children who are homeless or at risk of being so. Respite care will be provided. *Second*, work with parents – a programme aimed at opening up a new way of seeing and working with children that will enable parents (almost exclusively mothers) to move away from the ever-present danger of child abuse. Workers will need to learn how to support but not intrude, help parents to solve problems, but not attempt to do it for them. Training will be provided in budgeting, resumé writing, effective job-seeking, assessing services for food, clothing, housing, medical needs. *Third*, the setting up of a business – surplus profits will support the first two areas of activity, e.g. a thrift shop, restaurant, corner market.

We hope to strengthen 'family literacy' with festival celebrations and time spent together in daily life activities such as meal preparation and gardening. Each mother will spend time in the daycare facility to learn about child development and healthy parenting, and to enrich her own life. Some mothers will take our daycare training which qualifies as an accepted programme for the state welfare-to-work programme.

Mothers grow through the work we do together. They become healed by this healing education. With the children – in particular small children – it is much more possible to bring healing to those hurts that came at a tender age. We can see the healing as the children learn to play. When they first come to our programme they do not play at all. About a third of the children have been sexually abused, and these children are under five. It is very upsetting. Many of them have been terribly physically abused in addition to being moved from place to place – having no place to call home. They have strained relationships with their mothers, because the mothers are themselves under a tremendous strain. That is why having the mother in there too is really important. They can leave all that at the door for a while.

A Waldorf-inspired nursery/kindergarten is homelike in its protection and pace, a quality that is very important to the children who have been or are homeless, and have a great need for a homelike environment for their healthy development.

(Carol Cole, The Sophia Project. For further information or to offer support contact: email SophiaProjaol.com)

In South Africa a visiting tutor shares teaching skills with Waldorf teacher trainees.

Chapter 10

Organization of the Global Waldorf Early Childhood Movement

The one and only reality befitting the present age would be to overcome and eradicate nationalism and for people to be stirred by the impulse of the universally human.

Rudolf Steiner, *Festivals and their Meaning*

Local Diversity, Global Community

The extent, breadth and versatility of this movement is one of its most striking features – and is quite unique in the history of early childhood education. Waldorf early childhood centres are to be found in almost every corner of the globe, with each setting both reflecting and serving the culture in which it stands, yet sharing a common intention with other Waldorf early childhood initiatives worldwide. It is truly a modern multi-cultural movement in every sense.

Although each early years centre and school will share the same pedagogical principles and understanding of child development, there is the freedom for each teacher to bring fresh inspiration and creativity to the expression of these intentions. The cultural setting for the school may also express itself, and the needs of each child can be given consideration. Thus each school or kindergarten has at once both unique and universal characteristics, and the education continues to review its practice and evolve new forms to meet changing social conditions. The delicate balance and creative edge between valuable continuity and healthy innovation are constantly being explored.

Within each country an association of Waldorf early childhood initiatives is usually formed. These associations support teacher training, ongoing in-service training through regional and national conferences, the recognition, registration and monitoring of standards of their member groups, and all issues relating to the growth and quality of Waldorf early childhood education.

The International Association of Waldorf Kindergartens

Together with these national structures there exists an international organization. In the following extract from 'An Overview of the Waldorf Kindergarten' (a publication of the Waldorf Kindergarten Association of North America) Dr Helmut von Kügelgen describes the beginnings of this association of Waldorf early childhood representatives from various countries:

'By the end of the 1960s a slogan rang forth around the world that the education of the young child makes a life-long impression on the human being's destiny, and educational issues became the headlines of the newspapers. Among parents, one could see an unprecedented uncertainty because of the prevailing opinion of educational theorists who could only envision a cognitive education for the future, supported by audio-visual media.

The opposite extreme, an anti-authoritarian education, in which the children did not work on the necessary conditions for life and development, soon showed its destructive effects. This challenged Waldorf education to work for a healthy education, for a sheltered and guided childhood, and also to work against early cognitive education in the first seven years. Waldorf pre-

school educators discussed in the press and at meetings of representatives of the new pedagogy what they had been practising in Waldorf kindergartens for many years.

In many lectures, meetings and conferences, kindergarten teachers, school teachers, doctors and scientists worked together to set forth the conditions of childhood. Brochures and leaflets were printed in which the developmental stages of the child were presented and learning through imitation was described. Such imitation assumes that the kindergarten teacher is doing sensible, practical life activities in the kindergarten. Themes were discussed, such as free play, simple toys, speech development through the example of the educators, story-telling and puppet plays, and artistic activities in music, movement and handwork; there were also discussions about the social and moral qualities in the group life of children and in the work with parents.'

Out of this work there came together, in 1969, 24 German institutions which formed an Association of Waldorf Kindergartens, whose greatest concern is to struggle responsibly for the rights of children to a human education. With the effort to create the legal papers for this Association, the necessity arose to work together with Waldorf kindergartens in other countries – so the Association soon expanded with the agreement of the Steiner Waldorf kindergartens of many lands. From its very founding, one of its purposes was to intervene on an international scale against educational theories which still today threaten the healthy development of the young child through one-sided cognitive pedagogy.

This union named itself the 'Internationale Vereinigung der Waldorf Kindergartens'. Its board of directors consists of members of many countries, and it provides a continuing exchange of experience across borders. It is concerned with establishing and developing a kindergarten education and the corresponding work with the parents, which suits the human being's development, and preserves the creative forces found in the growing child and allows them to ripen.

The Association reflects a strong world-wide co-operative spirit within the movement. In certain instances an established kindergarten in one country will 'adopt' a new centre in an area which may have little in the way of resources – sending money, equipment and often teachers to support the early beginnings. Teacher trainers will travel to other countries to make an input into teacher education. Such part-time training courses have been set up in India and the Far East, with experienced teachers and trainers travelling from America, Australia, the United Kingdom and Europe to share their knowledge and experience. Frequently students have taken up training in courses abroad before returning to their own countries to begin the first Waldorf kindergarten.

In 1955 an annual international Waldorf kindergarten conference was set up in Hannover, Germany, with encouragement from Klara Hattermann, who had worked with Elizabeth von Grunelius, the first Waldorf kindergarten teacher (see Chapter 11). In addition, a second annual international conference takes place in another nominated country. These conferences can attract close to a thousand participants from across the globe. Every seven years an international gathering takes place at the Goetheanum in Switzerland.

Waldorf early childhood education provides a range of settings from daycare (both home- and centre-based), parent and child groups, kindergartens with mixed age groups, from three to seven years, and parent-support programmes. In recent years work has begun with an international working group exploring issues of daycare (see Appendix 1) and issues affecting the healthy development of children (see Appendix 3).

Moral Development and Respect for Diversity and Difference

Burnum Burnum 1936 - 1997. The Universal Human

In 1938, as members of the Australian Anthroposophical Society prepared for the country's bi-centenary celebrations, they turned their attention and studies towards ancient Aboriginal spirituality. Into this mood of openness came the aboriginal Burnum Burnum. As a child he had been taken from his mother by social workers, becoming one of the 'lost generation' of aboriginal children. He went on to become an author, actor and activist for the rights of his people.

He joined the Society and established deep mutually meaningful relationships with a number of Australian Anthroposophists and Waldorf educators. He often referred to the potential of Waldorf education for restoring the self-esteem of aboriginal children and preserving and embracing their natural spirituality. His love of both the didgeridoo (Aboriginal musical instrument) and Mozart seemed to symbolise his ability to embody 'the universal human' and the transcendance of cultural and racial divisions.

The diversity of Waldorf education is a notable characteristic, and one that gains increasing significance and respect with the contemporary concern for equality of opportunity. Its ability to transcend cultural barriers rests upon a number of elements which promote a quality of universal relevance and tolerance.

It is the view of Waldorf educators that tolerance cannot be taught in the same way as, for example, history. Tolerance is closely aligned to morality, and this education has an approach which cultivates and emphasizes moral development within the child. In the kindergartens, social, behavioural and interactive skills are developed through creative play, and respect and reverence are fostered by *the entire mood* of the kindergarten experience. These qualities lay a foundation for the continuing moral emphasis of the education throughout the following school years when, additionally, the child will gradually be led to a more conscious awareness of human diversity through the Waldorf curriculum. In the kindergarten, with such a young age-group, it is not so much the 'details' of diversity which are addressed but the human qualities which lay the foundation for the acceptance of individual differences.

If *respect and reverence* are experiences in the everyday life of the young developing human being, then the power and capacity to act and behave appropriately in the social sphere are developed within them. From this inner attitude children can awaken to the need to respect and recognize *a common humanity*, transcending differences and creating a meeting point; and this common humanity finds expression in the individual 'I'.

The education aims to strengthen individuality, and most significantly to develop an *ethical individualism*, a characteristic which enables recognition of one's own individuality and the individuality of the other, in such a way that we can meet as individual to individual, 'I' to 'I', an activity which goes above and beyond differences.

A further element which allows the international, cross-cultural nature of Waldorf education to flourish is the common thread of the pedagogical aims and principles. This common thread behind all Waldorf initiatives has given birth to a remarkable mood of co-operative working across the world.

Economics and Accessibility

As will be discussed in the following chapter, the first Waldorf school was funded by the profit from Emil Molt's factory, but it was not long before the factory itself met financial difficulties, to some extent because of its funding of the school; and inevitably it evolved into a school available to those who could pay. The economic question still remains the fundamental practical problem for Waldorf education today. How can this gift of Rudolf Steiner's social and educational vision be made accessible to those children whose parents are unable to pay for it? How can parental freedom of choice be respected if money remains an obstacle? The argument for the integrity and value of pluralism in education is constantly being championed by Waldorf educators; in some countries it is met with respect and a practical, helpful response, while in other countries it notably fails to find fertile ground.

This challenge has a particularly poignant note, for this form of education – with its commitment to the development of self-identity and self-esteem, respect for individual destiny and individual freedom, a rich and comprehensive understanding of human development, and a non-denominational, holistic, comprehensive intention – has an intrinsic *therapeutic* aspect, and is therefore of particular value to children who are born into deprived circumstances. In early childhood, the steady, reassuring rhythmical nature of the kindergarten experience, the home-like environment, and the opportunity for creative play, have much to offer children who are experiencing anxiety and stress-related symptoms. In 1994 UNESCO made the following statement on Waldorf education:

> *'Education in critical environments: The originality of this educational approach and its long-standing practical application all over the world have recently proved to be particularly interesting and fruitful in such disadvantaged environments as slums, refugee camps or in conflict situations – conditions where alternative channels of education often prove to be more efficient than official school systems. The following pilot projects are outstanding examples of the success of this alternative method, and they might be of great benefit to other situations and countries:*
>
> - *Soweto and Alexandria (South Africa) – schools in various black townships and integrated schools*
>
> - *Shoat refugee camps (Gaza strip) – a Waldorf kindergarten and remedial education for Palestinian children*
>
> - *Zagreb (Croatia) – a Waldorf kindergarten*
>
> - *Favela Monte Azul, Sao Paulo (Brazil)*
>
> - *Holywood, Belfast (Northern Ireland), where Protestant and Catholic children are taught together*
>
> - *Pine Ridge Reservation, South Dakota (USA), a school for Sioux Indian children.'*

A striking phenomenon in the recent development of the movement has been a rejuvenation of the original impulse for the founding of the first Waldorf School (see Chapter 11). In many situations across the globe, Waldorf teachers are struggling with great courage and determination to find ways to meet the needs of children who have been born into difficult conditions. The reports in the previous chapter represent just a few such centres, working at the heart of the social environment and giving practical substance to Rudolf Steiner's challenging and profound Social Ethic:

The healthy social life is found when in the mirror of each human soul the whole community finds its reflection and when in the community the virtue of each one is living.

Chapter 11

Our Historical Roots

The First Waldorf School

I felt the tragedy of the working class; to be held back by lack of money from sharing in the education of the rich middle class. I also had a sense of what it would mean for social progress if we could support a new educational endeavour within our factory...it seems to me that the true birthday of the Waldorf School was April 23rd, 1919. On this day Rudolf Steiner gave a lecture to the workers in the Waldorf Astoria factory....

Emil Molt, *Emil Molt and the Beginning of the Waldorf School Movement*

Emil Molt and Rudolf Steiner

The first Waldorf school was opened in Stuttgart, Germany, on the 7th September 1919, with some 250 pupils. This school was established as an initiative of Dr Emil Molt, the managing director of the Waldorf Astoria cigarette factory. The title 'Steiner Waldorf' acknowledges the collaborative effort of these two men in sowing the seed for what was to become the largest independent school movement in the world, based upon common pedagogical principles. The name 'Waldorf' is a reference to the southern German village of Walldorf in Baden, the home of the founders (the Astors) of the original factory.

In his autobiography, Emil Molt outlines the steps that led to his productive relationship with Rudolf Steiner. Both Molt and his wife Berta had been actively seeking a satisfying alternative to the popular theories of Haeckel and Darwin. In 1902 Emil attended a lecture by members of the Theosophical Society in Stuttgart, and later, at a friend's recommendation, he was also present at a lecture given by Steiner in the same year. From that point, Anthroposophy became their path of personal development and they joined the Anthroposophical Society. Significantly, Berta and Emil Molt were to offer practical support and advice to the group involved with the financial aspects of the building of the Goetheanum in Dornach; indeed, it was Molt who suggested the name 'Goetheanum'.

The Threefold Social Order

Emil Molt never missed any of the lectures Steiner gave in Stuttgart, and he soon became familiar with Steiner's views on the need for social renewal after the devastation of the First World War. As a socially minded entrepreneur, Molt had been interested in new social forms which were being explored in Germany after the war. He shared these possibilities with Steiner, who emphasized the need for more radical solutions, which he called *the Threefold Social Order*. On 12th February 1919 Steiner published these ideas for social reform under the title *Toward Social Renewal*. In his autobiography, Molt later commented, 'I was deeply impressed that he was able to reinterpret and revitalize the French revolutionary principles of liberty, equality and fraternity which had become such empty catch-phrases. He paired liberty with a free spiritual life, equality with human rights, and fraternity with economic life. This book became my constant guide in all questions of social life.' Molt spearheaded a large-scale appeal in Germany, Austria and Switzerland which initially attracted an enthusiastic response.

Steiner's vision embraced three independent but co-operating spheres of human activity – the economic, political/human rights, and the spiritual/cultural. The ideal of brotherhood would guide economic matters; the principle of equality would inform political decisions, and freedom would be maintained in all issues relating to the spiritual and cultural realms.

The essential thought behind this vision was that of freedom balanced by ethical individualism within each sphere of activity, although there would be an interdependent, mutually supportive relationship between the three. Steiner believed that education (belonging to the free spiritual/cultural sphere of human experience) should be independent of state control and economic interests.

The independence from outside interests arising from such freedom has present-day relevance, with increasing political involvement in education in certain countries, and with decisions affecting education being made from a political centre rather than from within the educational sphere itself. What should be educational questions are then in danger of being linked to political or economic interests – which to Steiner was a cause for great concern. He believed that those actively involved in teaching and with the necessary pedagogical knowledge should be responsible for decisions concerning their profession, as these decisions should arise from the insights gained with direct teaching experience.

The first steps

In promoting these ideas, Emil Molt had been providing adult education classes for his own employees, and from this experience he began to form the idea of providing education for children.

Molt became aware that the gifted child of one of his workers would be prevented from proceeding to higher education because of his family's limited financial means; so he put the idea of a school to his employees, who enthusiastically embraced the possibility. Molt then approached Rudolf Steiner with the proposition, and asked him to plan, organize and supervise a school for the children of his factory workers.

It is clear that the original impulse behind the foundation of this school movement was social in nature, born out of Molt's deep interest in social issues – particularly those of equality of opportunity for all. As he himself noted, 'The original idea which led to the founding of the school was a social one, to provide the children of workmen and employees with the same teaching and education as that enjoyed by families of means'.

Molt himself offered the first financial contribution of 100,000 marks from his factory's profits – thereby demonstrating one of the tenets of Steiner's Threefold Social Order, that the economic sphere would support the cultural/educational realm whilst respecting its freedom. The Cultural Minister of Stuttgart supported the venture and declared himself willing to respect the autonomy of the teachers. He particularly appreciated the fact that an industrialist was using his profits to establish a school which in turn would be offered free of charge to workers' children.

The school is founded

In August 1919 Steiner began an introductory teacher's course. The content was subsequently published as *The Study of Man* (recently republished by the Anthroposophic Press as *The Foundations of Human Experience*) and *Practical Advice to Teachers* – both still fundamental texts for Waldorf teacher trainees. At the very beginning the teachers were employees of the Waldorf-Astoria company, and were paid according to needs. The following year they expressed the need for a review of the school's organization which would reflect their role as an expression of the 'free spiritual life' in accordance with the vision of the Threefold Social Order (the school was called 'The Free School' to reflect this principle.) Moreover, the children of the company's employees were now only a small proportion of the total student number, and Molt could not indefinitely carry the financial demands of the growing school. A Waldorf School Association was founded in May 1920.

Before long the school was educating over a thousand children, and Waldorf schools appeared throughout Germany, Switzerland, Holland, England, Norway and the USA. Today, the original Waldorf school site is home to a teacher training college, eurythmy school, research institute, school, and branch of the Anthroposophical Society.

Emil Molt continued to support Anthroposophical activity, being particularly interested in finding practical ways of putting into operation Steiner's suggestion that profits from commercial enterprise should be used to enable spiritual and cultural activity. Although these intentions met with considerable difficulties, a number of significant ventures still exist today – Weleda (whose products are sold in many health food shops today), the Arlesheim clinic – and, most impressively, the global Waldorf school movement.

The Molts were witnesses to the destruction by fire of the first Goetheanum in 1922, and were present at Steiner's funeral in 1925. In 1929 the Waldorf-Astoria factory was sold and subsequently closed. In 1920 Steiner had asked Emil Molt directly to become responsible for a threefold approach toward social reform. He had carried this request to the best of his ability, and with many hardships. Although in 1921 Steiner himself acknowledged that prevailing conditions meant this activity could not proceed successfully, Molt's efforts bore lasting fruit, and his name will always be associated with the founding of the successful Waldorf school movement. He had embodied Steiner's ideal of the power in the individual's freedom to take initiative.

By the time of Steiner's death another school had been established in Germany, one in the Hague, and another in England. The movement grew steadily, and by the Second World War, some 16 schools had been opened, until Hitler closed down all of the Waldorf schools, clearly threatened by the qualities of self-esteem and individual liberty which they sought to foster.

By 1933 Molt was in poor health. The Nazis insisted that the curriculum content should be changed if the school were to remain open, and the teachers refused. On 16th June 1936 Emil Molt died without having to endure the experience of his beloved school being closed by decree in March 1939. The school eventually reopened in 1946.

From acorn to oak....

From this relatively modest beginning, the Waldorf movement has spread throughout the world, and the demand for this unique education continues to grow all over the globe. In certain countries, like The Netherlands and Germany, Waldorf schools are to be found in every major town. Elsewhere, because of the prevailing educational or political climate, these schools face financial and practical obstacles to their well-being, despite increasing parental demand for Waldorf education.

Waldorf schools are fully or partly state-funded in places – for example, Finland, New Zealand, The Netherlands, Germany and Norway. Other countries, such as England, are exploring ways to gain funding which would respect their freedom to stay true to their own curriculum and pedagogical principles. It continues to be a source of great frustration for teachers and parents that the ideal of social inclusion cannot be met, due to insufficient, or non-existent, government support. Many schools and individuals have attempted to develop innovative and courageous solutions to the problem, involving considerable sacrifice on the part of teachers and parents. These efforts often lead to the strengthening of community, and what is missing materially is often balanced by renewed determination to find ways to provide this form of education for children.

The movement is now international and inter-cultural and continually demonstrates its capacity to create fresh forms of expression to meet the needs of its surroundings. At the beginning of the new millennium there were some 1500 early childhood centres, 780 schools, 60 teacher training centres, and many curative initiatives, in over 30 countries.

The First Waldorf Kindergarten

How does life become play and activity in the kindergarten so that eventually a metamorphosis will become realized: so that in adult life, work and social activity will acquire the same intensity and love of action which was present in the child's play?'

Rudolf Steiner to Elizabeth von Grunelius
(from material in the Goetheanum archives)

Rudolf Steiner and early childhood education

The first Waldorf school in Stuttgart did not have an early childhood department, and the first Waldorf kindergarten was not established until 1926, one year after Rudolf Steiner's death. This has sometimes been interpreted as meaning that Steiner himself did not wish to include early childhood in his educational vision, and that the kindergarten movement has arisen in response to subsequent social needs. In fact, quite the opposite is the case, for Steiner had openly expressed frustration at the lack of such a facility.

In his early lectures (in *The Study of Man*) to the first group of teachers, he expressed concern that education was only beginning after children had passed through the sensitive age of imitation (birth to seven years) – a time when the child would already have been deeply affected by the quality of care she had experienced. In the same passage he refers to the need for a partnership between parents and teachers in the care of the young child, a still enduring characteristic of Waldorf kindergartens today: 'Our intention will only be fully accomplished when we, as humanity, will have reached the stage where parents, too, will understand that special tasks are set for humankind today, even for the first years of the child's education'.

Steiner's classroom observations awakened his awareness that, by school age, many obstacles could already have been placed in the path of healthy child development. He also made reference to the particular significance of the child's experiences in early childhood for development at a later stage. He was heard exclaiming, 'We need kindergartens! We need kindergartens!', and made the following statement at a teacher's conference:

'It is true that it would be better if you could have the children in the kindergarten. The longer you have them, the better. Thus you could admit children who are not yet old enough to come to school. Until now, we have been essentially admitting children at the same age that they normally go into the public elementary school. We begin with them only after the age of imitation is over. It would be very nice if we could bring in some children in the first seven years of early childhood education. In the end, we must have them somewhat younger, it is much less important when they are older.'

In 1921, in reviewing the early beginnings of the Stuttgart school, he had remarked:

'Whenever one approaches the very young child in the role of an educational leader, through parenthood, or another relationship, one feels to an extraordinarily strong degree the duty to be able to enter into the entire course of human life with understanding. For that reason, it has always been particularly painful for me that we have been able to receive in the Stuttgart Waldorf school only children who have already reached the necessary age, as designated in Middle Europe, when one enters school. It would gratify me deeply if the younger child could also be accepted into the Free Waldorf School. But irrespective of other difficulties, the establishment of some type of school for young children is principally obstructed by the fact that we suffer from an extraordinary lack of money in all areas of our anthroposophical movement. Due to this great lack of money the most we can hope for is that, if the Waldorf School isn't regarded in too hostile a manner in the future, the younger child will be accepted into it.'

(Rudolf Steiner, *Soul Economy and Waldorf Education*)

Elizabeth von Grunelius: 15th June 1885 - 3rd October 1989

Elizabeth von Grunelius and the first Waldorf kindergarten

In 1914 Rudolf Steiner met Elizabeth von Grunelius, a young woman of 19 from the Alsace region of Germany. She was working with a group of artists, which included Steiner himself, on the wood sculptures in the first Goetheanum, and she had already trained as a kindergarten teacher. She remained at the Goetheanum for 18 months, working and attending Steiner's lectures, before taking further teacher training in Berlin.

As he increasingly felt the urgent need to bring the young child into his educational framework, Steiner remembered his meeting with Elizabeth, and in 1920 invited her to found and develop an educational provision for early childhood. The Waldorf School was unable to provide a suitable space for the initiative: available space was being taken up as additional classes were added, and financial restraints were being felt as all funds were being directed toward building up the school – even though Steiner kept repeating that the kindergarten was more important.

Elizabeth von Grunelius joined the College of Teachers, and as kindergarten work was not at that point possible, she took up handwork and supply teaching between 1920 and 1926. She also returned to Dornach for a time to work with artistic activities – eurythmy, creative speech, modelling, painting and Anthroposophical studies, as preparation for her future kindergarten work.

In 1924, at Herbert Hahn's instigation, a space was created for a small hut within the school complex, a sandpit, and a garden. However, two more years passed before the kindergarten opened in Easter 1926, and so destiny determined that Rudolf Steiner (who died in 1925) was not present at the opening, and the teachers themselves had to take responsibility for carrying this new aspect of Waldorf education forward.

The fundamental principles for early childhood

Elizabeth von Grunelius had worked closely with Steiner in establishing the fundamental principles for Waldorf early childhood education. As early as 1906, in his extended essay 'The Education of the Child', he had already referred to the key words for the first seven years of childhood – *imitation and example*; and he would subsequently refer to these principles repeatedly, and in increasing depth. He went further to describe the natural inner attitude of the young child as being '*bodily religious*', a somewhat startling concept at the time. This refers to the child's intense engagement in physical activity, and their open surrendering attitude to their surroundings and all that takes place within their immediate environment.

Steiner pointed to the deep trust that was inherent in this characteristic of early childhood, and the responsibility of the adult toward this innate trust. In response to questions concerning the actual practice of working with young children, Steiner's response was that the teacher should consider everything which could be brought into the sphere of imitation. The second aspect of preparation was to be the teacher's *own* engagement in artistic work, for this would awaken his understanding of particular aspects of the child's development.

He recommended *modelling*, on the basis that its forming experience of curves and planes helped develop a sensitivity to the formation and development of the physical body; *music* would develop an openness to the feeling side of human development; whilst *speech training* would allow a connection with the 'I' experience within each human being. To this day, all Waldorf training courses contain a strong element of artistic training in order to awaken this consciousness within the teachers themselves. Time and time again, throughout her teaching career, Elizabeth

Elizabeth von Grunelius's subsequent activity

For 12 years Elizabeth continued to carry forward the kindergarten work in Stuttgart, until the school closed in 1938. Very few teachers observed in her kindergarten, but Klara Hattermann was a rare exception, and this relationship later formed a bridge to other kindergarten teachers.

In 1940 Elizabeth was invited to America to open a kindergarten in Kimberton, which eventually became the Kimberton Farm Waldorf School; and she also helped to establish a school on the campus of Adelphi College. During a sabbatical year in 1947 she returned to Europe, and gave support to Klara Hattermann and a few German and Middle European kindergarten teachers who were expanding the work. In 1954 she founded a kindergarten in Chatou, France, and by this time she had pioneered kindergartens in three languages (German, English and French).

She began to give active support to conferences which enabled the early pioneer teachers to go more deeply into the fundamental aims and principles of the work, and to develop its practical aspects. In 1954 she returned to Europe, and soon moved from Stuttgart to Dornach. The first international Waldorf kindergarten conference in Hannover began in 1951, and although no longer a practising teacher she took an active part in this aspect of the work. The founding of the International Association of Waldorf Kindergartens in 1969 (see Chapter 10) gave the work an international focus point, and she was regarded as honorary chairperson.

Final years

After 33 years of international meetings, a conference for Waldorf kindergartens world-wide was organized at the Goetheanum at Easter 1984. Elizabeth von Grunelius was in her 89th year – the last remaining teacher of the original Waldorf College of Teachers – and she took part in all the meetings of that historical gathering. Toward the end of her life, when the participants of the annual international conference in Hannover numbered almost 900, she always sent her greetings, eventually dictating them when her eyesight failed. The last two years of her life were spent in a residential home in Schopfheim. Up until a year before her death in 1989 she continued her artistic activities. Two days before her death, at the age of 94, she visited Dornach for the last time, the place where her extraordinary destiny as the founder teacher of this vast movement had begun, at the age of 19.

Early Childhood Education and the Waldorf School Plan *(1950)*

In 1950 Elizabeth gave practical examples for Waldorf kindergarten work in her seminal book *Early Childhood Education and the Waldorf School Plan*, an American publication. A second version was published in England in 1955 under the title *Educating the Young Child*. The book explored the fundamental Waldorf principles of imitation and example, the child's sensitivity to sense impressions, and the importance of play. She named three aspects of Waldorf early childhood education:

- kindergartens should become places where children are protected from the harmful influences of 'our highly intellectual age';

- Waldorf education can find roots anywhere as it rests upon an understanding of 'what is universally and fundamentally human'; and

- the education rests on this understanding only, and therefore allows space for 'the ever fresh initiative of individual teachers'.

A particular challenge was that Rudolf Steiner was not able to observe in the first kindergarten, or give direct leadership to the development of the kindergarten movement. Perhaps this has meant greater responsibility yet also more freedom for Waldorf early childhood teachers in the deepening and reviewing of their understanding of Steiner's original indications. Today the teachers still recognize the need both to explore the expression of these fundamental principles in ways that are relevant to the times in which they live – sensitive to the various cultural environments in which they find themselves working – and to allow creative responses to the specific needs which they encounter.

This constant striving, ongoing review and deepening of understanding have enabled the movement progressively to evolve, and continuously to possess a freshness and relevance. The opening sentence in the preface to the original 'The Education of the Child' has a strikingly contemporary note, 50 years on: '*It is a characteristic of our time that, while the average life span of the human being become longer and longer, the span of childhood gets shorter and shorter*'. This statement from the first teacher of the first Waldorf kindergarten manages to articulate, at the start of a new millennium, the nature of the challenge now facing the teachers of what has become an international movement of 1,500 early childhood initiatives.

Chapter 12

The Life and Work of Rudolf Steiner (1861-1925)

That the spiritual world is a reality was as certain to me as the reality of the physical.

Rudolf Steiner's autobiography, 1923.

As will now be clear from earlier chapters in this book, Waldorf early childhood education is, then, part of the world-wide Waldorf educational movement, which provides a comprehensive, non-denominational, co-educational experience for children from, approximately, the age of three to eighteen or nineteen. Austrian scientist and philosopher Dr Rudolf Steiner's philosophy is referred to as Anthoposophy, from the Greek words 'anthropos', meaning humankind, and 'sophia', meaning wisdom – reflecting its efforts to penetrate and reveal the mystery of human existence. Waldorf education, together with a curative stream of special education (known as Camphill communities), is currently the most well known of the activities inspired by Steiner's work. His philosophy also provides the inspiration for an extraordinary range of practical initiatives – biodynamic agriculture, medicine, therapies, architecture, finance, social work and the creative and performing arts.

Steiner's Early Life

Rudolf Steiner was born on 27th February 1861 into a family of humble means, in a Slavic area rather than in a German-speaking culture, on the border between East and West – a biographical

Rudolf Steiner (1861-1925)
Reproduced with kind permission of the Philosophisch
Anthroposophischer Verlag, Goetheanum, Switzerland.

detail which was to find reflection in his life's work. A sister and a brother were to follow. Steiner's early childhood was spent in the small, rural peasant community of Pottschach. During this period he experienced the first of a number of polarities which were to become the focus of attention throughout his life.

On the one hand he was deeply immersed in nature because of the rural surroundings, and in his autobiography he emphasizes the effect this had upon his development. He helped with farm work, roamed in the forest, and responded to the peace and beauty of the natural environment. On the other hand he was exposed to technology, industry and science through his father's railway work. These two worlds – nature and science – were to remain lifelong interests.

Such contrasting experiences gave rise to another polarity that roused Steiner's interest. He was aware from an early age that there was a vast range of experience beyond physical, material reality. The visible, as represented by the world of science and matter, and the invisible spiritual world, were to become as much a source of inspiration for his later initiatives as was his interest in both the inner and outer experiences, and the wholeness of the developing human being.

Until early adolescence he lived uneasily with his inability to articulate his experience of this invisible reality. By the age of 13 he was interested in science and mathematics, and it was while studying geometry that he had what he later described as a breakthrough. A teacher had allowed him to borrow a book on geometry. This led to the revelation that these geometrical forms did not exist in outer reality but had been produced inwardly, in the mind, independent of outer sense experience; and yet one could speak of them with conviction. From this experience he came to understand the existence of an inner soul-space. He felt he could now find a way to give expression to his experience of the invisible, to articulate and differentiate between things that were sense-bound, 'seen', and things that were sense-free, i.e. 'not seen.' He described this release as his first real experience of happiness. He had taken a first step toward a destiny that required him to speak of a world of experience which embraced all that 'one does not see'.

Along with nature and science, other influences emerged in his youth – influences which were to continue as a motif in his later life. The same teacher who opened his awareness to geometry also introduced him to artistic expression. In village life he observed community and social codes of conduct, and he noted the hierarchical order. The world of politics entered through his father's lively interest and participation in political debate with fellow railway employees.

Later Influences

He then moved to Vienna in order to continue into higher education. His interest in natural science, physics, chemistry and philosophy intensified. At that time the academic world was permeated with Darwin's theory of evolution, and Steiner struggled with two enormous questions – how to reconcile the prevailing scientific image of humankind's evolution with his own understanding of the spiritual nature of the human being, and how to apply the methods of scientific exploration to spiritual research.

At the age of 22 he discovered another way forward in the work of Johann von Schiller, who had in Steiner's view managed to offer a more acceptable and inspiring contribution to the image of humankind. Schiller acknowledged humanity as being influenced on one side by the sensory world – a sense-bound experience; and on the other side by the logical laws of reason – a mind-based experience. However, he posited an intermediate state of consciousness which he called an 'aesthetic disposition', and which does not surrender to either sense-bound or mind-based experience – and so brings something of a spiritual nature to physical reality. Later Steiner continually emphasized the importance of cultivating the artistic nature of the child throughout her education in order to offset a purely intellectual approach to the learning experience, and to bring a moral dimension to the child's development.

Steiner's autobiography reveals his time in the University of Vienna, during his twenties, to be one of cultural vibrancy, and he began to reveal his considerable intellectual capacity. The roots for many of his later initiatives are to be found in this period of his life. A significant friendship with Karl Schroer, a professor of humanities, led to Steiner's lifelong interest in Johann von Goethe, and he went on to edit Goethe's complete works. In the educational sphere, at the age of 15 he had tutored fellow pupils at the high school in Wiener-Neustadt, and he had chosen upper school teacher training as his course of study at the Technical University, specializing in mathematics, natural history and chemistry. In Vienna he tutored a ten-year-old boy with severe learning and behavioural difficulties with such success that the boy went on to become a doctor. This constituted a very important formative experience for Steiner.

A number of stimulating friendships extended his interest in philosophy, and he credits this time as the foundation of his major and profound work, *The Philosophy of Freedom*. His outer cultural and intellectual activities accompanied the continuing deepening and clarifying of his spiritual perspective on humankind's nature and evolution.

Between 1890 and 1897 he lived in Weimar, editing Goethe's works and coming into contact with the thoughts of naturalist Ernst Haeckel and the great philosopher Friedrich Nietzsche. In 1897 he then moved on to Berlin for a most significant phase of his life. He married a widow, Anna Eunike, who died in 1911. He became a progressive editor of a literary magazine and gave lectures at a Workers' College, mainly on political and social issues – interests which were to re-emerge later in his proposals for a Threefold Social Order (see Chapter 11).

The Founding of the Anthroposophical Society

Of particular significance during this time is his meeting with the Theosophists. He had come into contact with this group briefly both in Vienna and Weimar. He was at odds with much of their approach to spirituality, particularly the influence of Indian spiritual traditions. Certain members of the group were drawn to his ideas, notably Maria von Sivers, who was to become his second wife, and who encouraged him to explore the possibility of developing a spiritual path which would meet the true needs of Western culture while retaining the depth of Eastern religion.

These connections led to his accepting the role of General Secretary of a German branch of the Theosophical Society. He struggled to bring his own contribution to the Society's members, but his views on freedom and the need to develop an ethical individualism (individual freedom balanced by moral responsibility) were not readily accepted. During this time his reputation as a speaker grew, and he began to accept offers to speak in a number of European cities.

His Berlin years also saw the publication of the three fundamental texts of Anthroposophy – *Theosophy, Occult Science* and

Knowledge of the Higher Worlds. Maria von Sivers became responsible for the publication of the notes from his many lectures. It was clearly Steiner's destiny to bring something new to the spiritual life of Western culture. However, this inevitably created difficulties for his role within the Theosophical Society, despite his insistence from the beginning that he be able to maintain his independence. The points of difference accumulated, and Rudolf Steiner left the group and founded the Anthroposophical Society on 2nd February 1913, with an international membership. This Society established a centre – known as the Goetheanum – in the town of Dornach, near Basel in Switzerland. This is still the international centre for Anthroposophy.

Practical Initiatives

With the outbreak of the First World War, Steiner became increasingly concerned with social issues and with finding a possible solution to the impending chaos of war. His proposals for social renewal, embodied in his Threefold Social Order, failed to find strong support at the time, and Steiner himself laid them to rest in 1921. However, they were the seed for what was to become his most lasting legacy, the founding of the world-wide Waldorf school movement.

A further polarity inherent in Steiner's work deserves consideration. His deep interest in the physical and spiritual, inner and outer, seen and unseen, finds reflection in the many initiatives which have arisen, and continue to arise, from his inspiring vision. The inner meditative activity that is intrinsic to following the Anthroposophical path of spiritual development frequently finds expression in outward practical activity. The existence of a vast array of connected activities is perhaps the most striking characteristic for those coming to Waldorf education for the first time. The active side of Anthroposophy continues, seeking creative responses to contemporary needs, finding new forms in diverse cultures, yet originating from a unifying common source of inspiration. In farming, medicine, therapies, curative education, finance, artistic work and social initiatives, groups of people gather and strive to give the Anthroposophical understanding of humankind renewed and relevant outer forms.

It is not possible within the confines of this chapter to give a truly comprehensive account of Steiner's philosophy or a full account of the many initiatives which arose from his work; but whatever definition one forms of the man himself, one cannot help but be deeply impressed by the biography of an individual who began as a child born into such humble surroundings and yet, by the time of his death at the age of 64, had laid the foundation for a movement which at the beginning of a new millennium, over 75 years after his death, continues to grow, seeking new ways of responding to humanity's most urgent concerns in modern times.

APPENDIX 1

Waldorf Daycare

Since the early 1990s Waldorf early childhood educators have increasingly turned their attention to the many issues arising from the need for working parents to seek out-of-home care for their young children. Waldorf initiatives have arisen to care for the under-threes, each setting evolving to meet the particular needs of its community. Home-based daycare, daycare groups attached to existing Waldorf kindergartens and schools, centres addressing daycare as well as a wide range of related needs – parenting-skills courses, after-school care, adult education, family-like mixed age groups – whatever form the care takes, there is a common intention: an earnest striving to meet the true needs of the under-threes within the compromises inherent in away-from-home care.

Conferences are devoted to exploring not only the many practical issues but also the pedagogical aspects of working with this vulnerable age group, with its own unique developmental needs. As with the kindergarten groups, Waldorf daycare centres are concerned with the *quality* of the experience offered to both parents and children, and the intention that practical solutions rest on a deep understanding of healthy child development. In 1992 a working group was formed, within the International Association of Waldorf Kindergartens, to research this aspect of early childhood care and to act as a focal point for the growing number of international initiatives. The following reports address some of the issues involved in this most important work.

Waldorf Daycare for the Under-Threes – *Helle Heckmann*
translated by Jean-Paul Bardou

When we approach a baby, something quite special is called forth in every one of us. What actually is it that a baby arouses in us?

Irrespective of whether we are a parent or a teacher, having dealings with a little child gives us a chance to grasp the world anew. We are suddenly made aware in a new way of the sounds, the noise level in our environment. In fact, all our senses are sharpened, because we are deeply moved, and the instinct to provide protection comes alive in us. We want to give of our best, we want to take care of this small being who is so dependent on our protection. The child accepts us just as we are, regardless of what we do to it.

What a responsibility!

All parents have to take responsibility for how they treat their child: a responsibility which they bear 24 hours a day until, as an adult, the child can largely shoulder the responsibility for himself. No one else can do this for the parents, no one can relieve the parents of this responsibility. And the experiences the parents share with their children have significance and consequences that extend far into the future.

It is extremely important to endeavour to acquire understanding and respect for the relationship between parent(s) and child and their unique circumstances. That is why it is necessary to ask ourselves the major question, can people other than the parents look after the little child at all? Can I, as a professional teacher, take care of the child of these parents in the right way? The significance of family should not be underestimated, though nowadays support is often needed. If a child does not receive love and the right care, then it pines away – and in the worst-case scenario it even dies. *Can infant care be carried out professionally without damaging the soul life of the child?* This is the essential question when we take a small child into our care.

The modern cultural context of daycare

It is world-wide no longer a question of whether we want to do this – the direction modern culture is taking shows this only too clearly. Families are breaking up, and women are being drawn back into work. The decisive question is: *How do we do it?* How do we come to a conscious perception of this responsibility, bearing in mind the child's development in body, soul and spirit? How do we do justice to the tasks in the light of the altered circumstances within family and social norms, which are constantly subject to sweeping changes all around us? And how do we do justice to the fact that through our professional involvement we become part of the child's destiny?

Our children are shaped by their environment. However, the children's needs are the same as they ever were. To grow into this world takes time – plenty of time. How do we succeed in helping the child without desecrating the land of childhood? Nowadays most children spend more time away from home than at home. For many children today the daycare centre is the dependable, peaceful place where they can experience the basic functions of life, such as housework, daily meals and unstructured play in a social setting.

How do we shape up-to-date daycare centres that do justice to the needs of both children and their parents? How do we approach present-day children with all the physiological and psychological challenges with which they present us? How can we train professional carers, and continue to educate ourselves so that we become better examples, true servers, who say YES to life and to our fellow human beings? Those who work with infants are all too often isolated, and stand alone with their immense task – and with difficult economic conditions being more the rule than the exception.

The International Working Group, Infant Care Section of the International Association of Waldorf Kindergartens

We, the International Working Group for Infant Care, are presently a group of about ten women from different countries who established ourselves in 1992 as part of the International Association. We have met at least twice a year in different European locations to work together on this theme. Our starting point is the care and rearing of infants, a task with which we are all engaged on a daily basis. During these years we have increasingly formed world-wide contacts with initiatives which are seriously interested in the above themes and actively working with them. Since 1998 we have been considered members of the Medical Section in Dornach and on this basis there has arisen an interdisciplinary practice that has built a bridge between pedagogy, medicine and social work.

Where this work with infants is concerned there can be no rigid models or prescriptions. Every initiative is so dependent on the cultural background of the particular country, the potentialities of particular individuals and the given framework.

To sum up, we can say that the fundamental needs of the child are the same everywhere. But all that belongs to satisfying these needs varies in each case as much as does the strength of the enterprise. We have endeavoured to create an international network where we can exchange our practical experiences, throw light on one another's problems, and confer together as colleagues. This work is still in its 'infancy' – and the next big step will be simply to improve our practice.

In October 1999 a conference was held at the Goetheanum with Dr Michaela Glöckler of the Medical Section and the International Association of Waldorf Kindergartens. At the conference we successfully worked on the need for infant daycare outside the family, and on establishing and presenting to the public our interdisciplinary team work with all the professional groups which work with infants. We hope that this impulse can continue to thrive all over the world and be supported and carried by many people, so that in the future the work can be further developed and deepened.

The working group: Gabriele Claus, Michaela Glöckler, Helle Heckmann, Angelika Knabe, Hanne Looij, Ina v. Mackensen, Zilla Moerch Pedersen, Petra Thal

(translated from the Danish by C. Nielsen)

Contact for the group: The Infant Care Working Group, C/- The International Association of Waldorf Kindergartens, D-70188 Stuttgart, Heubergstrasse 18.
Tel (+49) 711 925740 Fax 711 925747
Inter.waldorf@t-online.de

Waldorf Daycare – One Teacher's Reflections

In Denmark it is quite natural for children under 3 to have constantly running noses – not to be ill, but not to be well either. They have the highest rate in institutions and their parents are those who work the most. Divorce rates within the first two years are very high and the result is a family structure where the child is split between several homes. For all these reasons, I wanted to create a place, a home for children, not an institution: a place where children feel safe and comfortable, where they are in contact with the same adults all the time (no alternating shifts), where daily life is built around an understanding of the child's true needs.

After a year, the two year old becomes a three year old and should move up to a kindergarten, but I felt uncomfortable with that – they could continue with me, and so I felt the need to set up a place for a mixed age group of children up to school entry, where the older children could learn empathy toward the younger ones, and where the younger children could look up to the older ones. In other words, a place where children could learn from one another. In this way siblings could remain together and the only child could learn to take care of younger children and show consideration for those other than herself.

That is how Nokken came to be a place for children from toddler to school age (7 years in Denmark). It is a wide spectrum to span pedagogically – but it is also a delightful challenge. We currently have about 25 children, with about three or four children in each age group. This creates the possibility of playing with younger or older children, depending on where each child is in its own development. Typically, the three to four year olds hesitate for a time before they take a big step into the world of fantasy and social life. There is room for that because our rhythm is adapted to all ages. They certainly don't have to grow up quickly.

After a year I found that taking care of children who cannot walk was simply too demanding to allow their integration into a large group – with the many meals, the more numerous nap times, the need for care and peace and quiet, as well as close contact with adults. The several physical developmental steps – rolling, crawling, sitting, attempting to walk – require a lot of quiet and comfort, which is difficult to attain in a large group. We simply couldn't meet the need in a responsible manner.

The composition of daily life is carefully thought out, depending on the composition of the group. We are located in a large city, and most children live in apartments. As already mentioned, many families are divided, and many don't have social networks. For these reasons, we mainly take children from the local area so that they can see one another outside kindergarten times. In this way, the parents can also assist one another in taking care of the children and also have some social life together.

We value physical development very much and place major emphasis on it. Nowadays, there are problems because of reduced physical activity, for children don't have the opportunities to move as much as they should. So every day, rain or shine, we all take a walk. We walk because all the children need to move. If we were just to stay in our wonderful garden, some of the children would just sit. Movement gives joy to life: the child learns to know its body's abilities, and develops self-confidence. Language comes with movement, which is why we don't have dedicated singing in a circle. We sing when we walk, with great joy! If the wind blows we sing wind songs, seasonal songs, and so on. Moving is fun; it creates appetite and results in a healthy tiredness.

We go to specific places, including large parks, and the walk takes about 20 minutes. We stay there for a while, and the children can play freely on the grass, in the trees and around the bushes. We adults bring along needlework, hand-weaving spindles, clothes that need mending and so on. We are located at specific places so that the children know where we are. They can thus play in the great confidence that they know where to go should the need arise. We try not to interfere too much in their activities. We also limit surveillance and constant comments about the children's behaviour. Of course, there are rules of behaviour; the children may disagree, but not bite, hit others, pinch or scratch!

Playing is the fundamental ingredient in our combined daycare/kindergarten. Playing is the jumping board toward social life. All the dramas that are necessary to become a human being can unfold of their own accord. Both the beautiful and the ugly side are being tried out in play, which deepens the understanding that there are other people in life, and that to be together with others one must show consideration. It is important to listen to those other than oneself. This has surely become a central issue in present-day kindergartens.

We return to the kindergarten around 10.30 a.m. and we are very hungry by the time we arrive back 'home' around 11 o'clock. The group is then divided: there are eight one to two year olds who are taken care of by two adults and occasionally a student. They have a little wooden house at the end of our garden. These little ones change clothes in peace and quiet, and eating is highly concentrated work! The older children – three to seven years – eat in the big house, where there is a livelier ambience.

We make very simple food at the kindergarten, from bio-dynamic products: rice on Mondays, oats on Tuesdays, millet on Wednesdays (all three of the latter items only boiled in water), home-made vegetable pate on Thursdays, and seasonal vegetable soup on Fridays. We consider that communal eating is an important opportunity for social gathering. All certainly eat with a great appetite! – and when the meal is finished the small children take a nap until about 1.30 p.m. and the older children hear a story. The five to seven year olds go out so that there can be fewer children in the garden, with an adult who chops wood, saws, carves, does some gardening and so on.

The three and four year olds are now inside for half an hour while an adult is cleaning and clearing, decorating window sills, or preparing for a seasonal festival. The children play with dolls, dress up, rest on a couch. After that, they go to the changing room where it takes a long time for them to put their coats on. They then play in the garden until a group snack around 1.30 p.m. and picking-up time between 2 and 2.30 p.m. The children are tired but happy, and there is still the opportunity to spend a little time with the parents before dinner and bedtime. The children are still their parents' children!

The work of the adults at the kindergarten and daycare is very practical, with three old houses and a garden of around 900 square metres, many apple trees, gardening beds, chickens, rabbits, not to mention wood stoves to be kept alight – all of which requires a considerable amount of work for daily life to function adequately. The children observe all this meaningful and necessary activity. Consequently, the basis for our pedagogical work is imitation, a quite natural part of daily life.

The children can play side by side with an adult who is taken up with her own work. The simple experience of how life's basic fundamentals happen, strengthens the child's own development and understanding of how life integrates. All this happens through *doing*.

A kindergarten as a home?

For me it is a sizeable task for teachers to relate to our daycare and kindergartens in this new way, extending our work to embrace the care of the under-threes. Because these children will spend more time in institutions than at home, the 'institutional' influence has a profound meaning for them. When the child is at home, he often goes to other places – to visit friends, to the gym etc. The parents' need to do their best to activate and stimulate the child brings about a very great level of stress for the latter, and the values of the home lose priority. It is important for me to assist parents as they recover the meaning of the value of the family. If parents and children don't experience a close-knit relationship during childhood, what will happen in later life? In the many divided families where the child lives between two homes, with new 'fathers', new 'mothers', new 'siblings' and the like, the kindergarten can provide a new dimension; it becomes the more stable 'home'.

It must be said that some parents need to work, and the kindergarten's short opening hours make it difficult for them. They have had to obtain reduced working hours from their workplace as well as more consideration for family life. They have deliberately chosen another way of life, with a reduction of pace and a lower material standard of living. This requires a definite, conscious choice.

When people ask me what is most difficult about working in this way, I must necessarily answer: the personal work on myself that enables me fully to meet others. Meeting the children is very uncomplicated, if I have done my homework well: to be well prepared for the daily tasks, as well as with stories, songs and reflections on the previous day. Meeting the parents, and my colleagues, is however considerably more complicated. It is a major issue for me to find out how we, strong individualists that we are, can want to meet and, through listening to each other, create a common vision of our work and relationships

(**Helle Heckmann** *works at the Nokken Waldorf daycare centre and kindergarten, Denmark. The above report is a description of her work, but it must be stressed that each daycare centre finds its own creative solutions and way of working according to its particular situation.*)

APPENDIX 2

Waldorf Parent and Child Groups

Not *all* mothers work, of course! Mothers or fathers who choose to stay at home to care for their families also have the need for support and encouragement for their valuable work. This decision is not always an easy one, and frequently involves considerable sacrifice, financially and socially, and the frustration of putting personal ambitions 'on hold'. In the times in which we live, with the pressure on mothers to return to work as soon as possible after the birth of a child, the decision to remain at home is also a courageous one which does not always attract the respect it deserves.

Giving encouragement and support for the valuable task of parenting has always been a central feature of Waldorf early childhood education. This intention was stated in the foundation statement of the International Association of Waldorf Kindergartens, and is given a variety of expression in Waldorf early childhood centres. Home visits, interviews, parent evenings, communal celebration of festivals, talks, workshops, parenting courses, childbirth preparation and shared work days are some of the many attempts to express support in an active way.

Many Waldorf kindergartens have opened parallel Parent and Child groups where mothers and fathers can come with their under-threes and share a common experience within a social setting outside the home.

'Freedom without Chaos!': Parent and Child Groups - *Richard House*

'Today's children are an endangered species.' So begins Eugene Schwartz's recent and important book *The Millennial Child*. Signs are all around us of adult-driven intellectual agendas and a hyperactive, materialistic culture impinging ever more relentlessly on the lives of children at ever younger ages. As I write, it has been reported that one quarter of British children under 4 have a television set in their bedrooms. Even relatively conventional neuroscientists, like Professor Susan Greenfield of Oxford University, are beginning to suggest that an increasing information technology may entail profound long-term risks, including 'the potential loss of imagination, the inability to maintain a long attention span, the tendency to confuse fact with knowledge, and a homogenisation of an entire generation of minds. These risks could even actually change the physical workings of the brain.'

Perhaps it is the extreme openness and vulnerability of young children to an over-intrusive culture that has recently led Parent and Toddler Groups to gain increasing recognition within the Steiner Waldorf movement. In September 2000 the Second National Parent and Child Conference was held at the Alder Bridge Steiner Waldorf School near Reading, UK. In the literature circulated with the conference details, the organizers (Dot Male and Kathy McQuillen) wrote: 'There is a growing recognition within the Steiner educational movement that Parent and Toddler work is extremely important – from little acorns do great oak trees grow! And that this work embraces a whole range of skills particular to working with parents and small children.' The conference discussed, among other issues, the development of a Parent and Toddler network, and the founding of a national newsletter and web site.

In the pre-kindergarten sphere early childhood educationalists routinely refer to a 'curriculum' for the under-threes. Conventional education is increasingly speeding up the learning process rather than allowing for a naturally unfolding and respected developmental experience.

How does the Steiner Parent and Child Group respond to such a disquieting cultural context? (I will use the term 'Parent and Child' to cover both parent and toddler and parent and baby groups.) Quite simply, the aim is to create an environment which, as far as possible, provides an antidote to the aforementioned damaging cultural forces, and which, instead, *nourishes the physical, emotional and spiritual growth of the young child*, providing an alternative context in which such growth is healthily and unhurriedly facilitated. I will describe one group's approach in creating such an environment, the 'Fir Cones' Parent and Toddler Group in Norwich, UK.

The 'Fir Cones' Parent and Toddler Group

The group opened in September 1998 in an old Victorian reading room before moving to a community centre. There is clearly a considerable demand for what we are offering, and by September 2000 we were opening four mornings a week with over 40 babies and toddlers attending, aged six months to about three-and-a-half years.

A typical Toddler Group session

The session runs from 9.30 till 11.30, and we need about an hour to set up the room beforehand. The children change into soft play slippers on arrival and the first period of 45 minutes is devoted to free unstructured play, with all the playthings being made of natural materials. Parents are busily involved with the specific craft activity of the day.

We make a 'river' of blue silk which is 'populated' with sea-shells, basket 'ducks', felt animals, a simple wooden boat. We also make up a little house with wooden clothes frames and cloths, and create a 'kitchen' beside it. Our nature table is in the corner, with fresh flowers, and is decorated according to the season. There is a definite and predictable rhythm to each session.

9.30 – 10.20 *Free Play.* Parents can stay with their children, socialize with one another, or join in with the craft activity on which the leader and assistant are also diligently working. The children are, of course, welcome to join this activity.

10.10 The assistant begins to prepare the snack at the meal-preparation table, and again the children's participation is welcomed. Soon afterwards we begin to sing our simple 'Tidy time' song and the parents and children tidy away the toys in preparation for our snack time. The 'imitation in action' is wonderful to behold as the young children co-operate willingly to tidy away. New parents have been known to look on in shocked incredulity when they first see this happening! – but, like the other parents, they're soon using it at home – and with considerable success.

10.30 Once the table is laid, often with children's volunteered help, we all gather for our snack. A short verse is spoken, a candle is lit and then we sing grace. The snack takes about 20 minutes –it is very positive for the children to begin to develop the fine motor co-ordination needed to spread honey or fruit-spread on their organic bread or rice cake (even though the table cloth usually needs a good wash afterwards!).

10.55 We sing our closing 'thank you' grace, and then it is time for the children and their parents to 'breathe out' by going out into our magical, walled and secluded garden. The children love this space – they run around, play hide and seek in the bushes, or simply sit and watch as the season 'plays out' in the lush vegetation and plant life. It is very useful to have access to a garden where the contrasting qualities of the seasons are so faithfully reflected. I play a pentatonic lyre in the garden, and if it hasn't been raining recently we carry out several full watering cans; the children love watering the plants and flowers – or playing with or watching with rapt fascination as the water emerges from the spout!

Soon we hope to set up a compost unit in the garden, and the children will then be able to see how we recycle whatever we can with nothing being thrown away or wasted if at all possible.

We go back into our room for our closing ring-time, with seasonal verses, songs, finger games, nursery rhymes and simple finger puppetry, in which both parents and children (voluntarily) participate, Sometimes the older, more boisterous children run around the room, but most often they freely choose to return and join in with our songs and verse.

We sing our 'goodbye' song together and then it's going home time (except for the leader and assistant, who spend 30-40 minutes clearing away).

From the parents' viewpoint

We recently circulated a questionnaire amongst our parents in order to gain insight into their experience of our group and to determine what parents were actually seeking from it. The following is a summary of their responses (anonymity was offered to all respondents, and all answers were entirely unprompted).

189

What aspects of a Waldorf Parent and Child Group do you value most for your child?

Replies:
- the calm atmosphere and the overall environment
- opportunities for social relationships
- the regular and predictable rhythm and structure of the sessions
- the opportunity to learn verses and songs
- the recognition of children's individuality
- recognition of the seasons and the natural world
- the simple wooden toys
- the thoughtfulness, the awareness, the recognition of our spirituality and the absence of junk food, noisy and garish plastic toys, and mayhem
- the freedom of the playtime, together with the structure of the snack and story times
- the lack of judgement or assessment of the children and the fact that the whole growth of the child is cherished
- the gentle welcoming atmosphere and the sharing of a meal and blessing

What aspects do you value for yourself as a parent?

Replies:
- the contact and companionship with like-minded parents and families
- the healthy and organic food
- the comfortable environment which allows me to 'let go' of my child and allow her more independent relationships
- the peace of mind that my child is safe in an environment where he is not pushed to conform to others' beliefs
- the shared craft activities and the opportunity to learn new craft skills

- the organization by the leader and assistant which allows me to be free to enjoy the session with my child
- the opportunity to talk to like-minded people about the dilemmas of bringing up a child, what to expose them to and what to protect them from
- learning new songs, new ways of doing things – e.g. snack time with its candle and song, which are also useful for the home

What characteristics of the experience do you feel are distinguishing features of a Waldorf Parent and Child Group?

Replies:
- more relaxed and relaxing, less chaotic than similar experiences
- the toys and general environment
- more regularity and structure, yet more freedom at the same time
- more parental involvement
- the care and thought which goes into every aspect of what happens
- the choice of songs and verses make sense
- the children are not over-stimulated or frenetic
- the quiet calm atmosphere
- a feeling of 'warmth'

Has your experience of the group encouraged you to find out more about Waldorf education and to perhaps consider moving on to a Waldorf school?

Replies:
- we are considering home education but if a Waldorf school became established in the area we would probably prefer this to home education
- we would love this, however we are unlikely to be able to afford it. We think it should be available to all

- we are home-educating and the group is a safe environment for our child to interact with other children
- the contact with the group encourages me to read more about Waldorf education

It became clear from the responses that Parent and Child Groups are as much for the parents as for the children. They are seen as providing a space in which a natural and healthy degree of independence of the child from the parent can begin to develop. For the parent(s) the isolation and intensity of being 'home-bound' is eased, and confidence in their role as parents grows as they converse with other parents and observe the group leader's way of relating to the children.

In my experience, Waldorf early childhood settings are distinctive and largely unique in their provision of an environment in which children learn the nourishing benefits of both unimpinged-upon freedom and individual creativity, and a clear, child-sensitive structure that invites co-operation and sociality. It is easy to create either formless chaos and mayhem or, at the other extreme, authoritarian over-regimentation – but far more subtle to create that most nourishing of spaces that lies 'between form and freedom'. It is the latter which the Waldorf Parent and Child Group at its best provides.

In a modernist culture in which the values of community are increasingly under siege, Steiner Waldorf education holds *the respect for community* as one of its central guiding principles. And this is indeed one of the most tangible aspects of Parent and Child Groups. Close friendships have developed between parents, and at the final summer term session (July 2000) the parents were arranging to meet up several times over the long summer break, creating a 'bridge of continuity' to the autumn term for their children – and for themselves.

Finally, from a strictly Waldorf educational viewpoint, a major function of Steiner Waldorf Parent and Child Groups is to act as a foundation from which a relatively easy and natural transition can be made into the Waldorf kindergarten. Many of the characteristics of the kindergarten, described fully in the rest of this book, will be reassuringly familiar to the Parent and Toddler Group child; and the more seamless the transition, the less the child will be subject to disorientating anxieties.

Rudolf Steiner was himself very emphatic that it is above all *the practical application and implementation* of his ideas that constitute the real test of their value and appropriateness. The feedback we received from parents indicates that the broad principles of early childhood Waldorf philosophy are eminently achievable within a pre-kindergarten setting. These gatherings of parents and children can create a refuge from the increasingly frenetic culture which surrounds and affects us all, and – not least – the impressionable young children in our care.

I would like to thank the following people who kindly helped with the questionnaire survey: Councillor Sam Allison, Dinah Berry, Tanya Brandish, Den Brinson-Hill, Sue Clarke, Selina Hamilton, Helen Kibblewhite, Zena Leech-Calton, Celia Little, Valentina Monguzzi, Clare Moss, Jenny Moy, Sabine Virani and Susanne Wardle.

*(**Richard House**, a trained Waldorf class teacher, leads the 'Fir Cones' Parent and Toddler Group for the Steiner Initiative in Norwich, England. This is a shortened version of a longer article, a copy of which is available from the author on request.)*

APPENDIX 3

The Alliance for Childhood

In 1999 the first step was undertaken toward establishing the Alliance for Childhood. Beginning with a small group of Waldorf educators, this association is now a forum for partnerships of individuals or organizations who work together out of respect of childhood in a world-wide effort to improve children's lives. The aims and objectives of this international alliance are:

- To fight poverty and neglect in all forms
- To work for better child health, physical and emotional
- To prevent commercialism aimed at children
- To reduce children's growing dependence on electronic media
- To improve childcare facilities
- To promote a play-based early childhood curriculum
- To strengthen family life

The Alliance views childhood as a responsibility to be shared by all citizens in a democratic society. It strives to create a focal point for reflection and action by people with vision and devotion who place child education and care within a larger social context. It works internationally, nationally and locally through:

- Exchanging information, research and experience to ensure co-ordinated action
- Promoting research and identifying conditions for healthy child development
- Creating a network of Alliance partners
- Collating regular reports from around the world
- Disseminating information through conferences, publications and the media

- Working with government agencies to influence change in laws and policies
- Forming local partnerships to promote the Alliance's aims and objectives amongst parents, child carers, educators, health care professionals and local government
- Encouraging joint activities between a range of community-based organizations involving children and adults

The following article by Colleen Cordes describes the initial impulse for this valuable new initiative – demonstrating as it does the desire of Waldorf teachers to respond to contemporary social needs and to form partnerships with non-Waldorf individuals and organizations who share the desire to speak up on behalf of children everywhere.

Forming an Alliance for Childhood - *Colleen Cordes*

As we enter a new millennium, is the very notion of childhood obsolete? Who, after all, really has the time in our fast-paced culture to let children be children? The idea that children are green young shoots, to be lovingly tended, shielded from social storms and financial droughts, and encouraged to take their own sweet time to bud and bloom... isn't that an outdated model for the Information Age?

Why can't we treat them instead as small programmable machines? Don't they come equipped, as a top Federal science official has suggested, with 'necktop computers'? Couldn't the speed and economic efficiency of their learning and growth be much improved by any number of technical improvements – plugging them into new electronic technologies, for example, or prescribing the right drugs to relieve the asthma, depression, hyperactivity, violence and other signs of stress from which they are increasingly suffering? Children must adjust to adults' schedules and priorities, right? – not vice versa.

Those were the questions ringing in the air in February 1999, at Sunbridge College (USA) as nearly 30 teachers, doctors, university professors, child advocates, and parents agreed to join together and boldly take up those very issues. They decided to work together as partners in forging a broad new international coalition to challenge the rush toward the ending of childhood.

The new partnership, called *The Alliance for Childhood*, will be open to all who value childhood, in its fullest sense, as the human potential to grow in wisdom and love. This potential is every child's sacred birthright, suggested Michaela Glöckler, a paediatrician and author of *A Guide to Child's Health*. But it's also a capacity shared by human beings of all ages, she added. And ultimately, keeping this ideal of childhood alive is essential to a healthy human future, the group agreed.

'What we share is a common reverence for the life of the child', said Kate Moody, executive director of the Open Gates Dyslexia Program at the University of Texas Medical Branch at Galveston. Christopher Clouder, chair of the International Council of Steiner Waldorf Schools, echoed the idea, adding that adults' respect for childhood ultimately reflects a respect for ourselves. 'There are qualities of childhood', Clouder explained, 'such as imagination, creativity, and a sense of play and wonder, that human beings should never outgrow or suppress. But it's these very qualities that are currently endangered at very young ages.'

Clouder and others in the group discussed the toxic mix of cultural, economic, and environmental transformations that are harming children around the world. One such threat to healthy childhood, many suggested, is the over-exposure of children to television, computers, and other electronic media. These tend to overwhelm their developing nervous systems, and to force them to deal with violence, sexuality, and other themes that even many adults find challenging. They also blunt the very powers of creativity and imagination – the ability, for example, to create brand new images in one's own mind – upon which future progress in science and technology itself depends.

The current focus on educational technologies is distracting schools, teachers, and parents from meeting students' real needs, added Lowell Monke, who teaches advanced computer technology for the Des Moines public schools. Adults, he said, now concentrate on buying children ever more powerful tools. Instead, they should be encouraging children to develop their own powers – especially the inner resources and human capacities they need in order to relate to, and care about, a troubled world. 'Our external tools are being substituted in all kinds of ways for the inner development of our youth – and not just our youth, of *all* of us', Monke added.

The group also pointed to documented increases in children's health problems, such as depression, violence against and by children, obesity, attention deficit disorder, and other learning disabilities. John D. Young, a physician and former head of the Laboratory of Molecular Immunology and Cell Biology at Rockefeller University, noted an unprecedented rate of chronic diseases among children in Asia, such as allergies and cancer. Young wondered whether this might be related to the sedentary lifestyles of an increasing number of children, which can block the expression of children's natural energies. Other environmental factors, such as pollution and stress, should also be considered, he added. 'It is clear to me that many chronic diseases should not happen in childhood, but we see them more and more', Young added.

Others expressed concern that many children suffer from too little time and attention from caring adults, too early an emphasis on intense academics, and from adults' obsession with quantitative tests of the intellectual abilities and achievements of young children. The latter two are counterproductive, mechanistic responses to the real school issue, suggested some members of the group. Educational problems are predictable, they said, when a culture treats its children as harshly as does ours.

John Taylor Gatto, former Teacher of the Year in New York, added that the current mechanistic approach to education is short-sighted. Creative responses to human mistakes, he argued, have historically been a major source of unexpected insights and experiential learning. Far from pressurizing young children not to fail, he suggested, we should be encouraging them to value trial and error as a fount of human wisdom. 'We are not machines' Gatto added 'So inadequacies and mistakes are to be desired. This is our birthright.'

And Bettyle Caldwell, former president of the National Association for the Education of Young Children, put it this way: 'What's really missing in American education is a certain gentleness'. Caldwell, now Professor of Pediatrics at the University of Arkansas for Medical Sciences, called for the Alliance to act as a 'community of conscience' working together to make the unmet needs of children a major social and political issue.

Children in many nations today also face even more extreme stress: civil and international wars that destroy homes and divide families, stubbornly high rates of poverty, and the loss of parents from AIDS. Even in affluent America, about one in five children still grows up poor, and an even higher number, rich and poor, suffer emotionally from the absence of a father or mother at home.

The damaging impacts of so many stresses on the young are being documented by researchers and noted by parents and teachers. The clear conclusion: however inconvenient for adults in a hurry, *children are still in need of the time and space to grow at their own pace*. In support of that goal, the new group agreed that each partner will continue his or her own ongoing efforts in support of children, but may now work in the name of the Alliance as well. Each partner will be able individually to initiate new efforts, in consultation with project co-ordinators, or to join together with other partners in the Alliance to serve on joint projects.

The coalition will also seek out other like-minded individuals and groups, and invite them to become partners in the new Alliance. Those attending the Sunbridge meeting described the new group as a 'soul alliance' which will be as decentralized as possible. Its shared commitment to the preservation of childhood will act as a kind of inner headquarters and 'heart' quarters. The partners agreed to create as little organizational bureaucracy as possible. Each partner will be free to contribute in his or her own way to the shared goals of practical action on the problems that threaten childhood.

The founding partners of the new Alliance – most being seasoned professionals in their 40s and 50s – ended the two-day meeting with an unusually childlike exercise of their own. Standing at a blackboard with chalk at the ready, Joan Almon, co-chair of the Waldorf Early Childhood Association of North America, issued a challenge to the rest of the group: 'what exactly is it that we want to protect for childhood?'. There was a brief silence. Then, Barry Sanders, grey-bearded Professor of English and the History of Ideas at Pithier College, mediaevalist and author of the provocative book *A is for Ox: Violence, Electronic Media, and the Silencing of the Written World*, bravely plunged into the lull with a simple but powerful trio of ideals. '*Joy, and love, and freedom!*', Sanders sang out.

Marilyn Benoit, psychiatrist, secretary of the American Academy of Child and Adolescent Psychiatry, and Washington lobbyist for children's causes, was right behind him, putting her own idealism on the line: '*A sense of wonder*', Benoit volunteered.

From there the group was inspired. Everyone, it seemed, wanted to share their own high aspirations, for the best that childhood can offer. What followed was a wonderful, unexpected envisioning of the kind of paradise that the child in each of us longs for, and deserves. The rights of children to grow at their own pace, to live intimately with the rest of the natural world, to make mistakes, and to have their special physical, cognitive, and emotional needs met – for their own sakes, as individuals, and for the sake of a healthy human future – all ended up on the long list of ideals that will guide the partners in their work together for the Alliance.

A short break followed. When the group came back together, Almon, herself inspired, shared with everyone an impromptu poetic version of the list, which she named 'Childhood', and everyone present pledged to contribute in some way to the new group's work in support of childhood.

At the end of the two-day meeting for the full Alliance, a smaller group met to consider one of the partner's first joint projects: how to respond to a growing emphasis on computers in pre-school and elementary education. As a task force, they decided to put together a package of supporting materials that will demonstrate why the emphasis on computers in educating young children is inappropriate (now formally published as *Fool's Gold* by the Alliance in late 2000 - LO). The package will include quotations and articles that have already been published, as well as a clear, well researched statement about healthy child development, the hazards that computers pose to such development, and alternative technologies that parents and schools can choose to nurture children in more age-appropriate ways. The latter include, for example, play, artistic activities, gardening, nature exploration, story-telling, and the low-tech power of a library card. Once the package is ready, the task force hopes to publicize it widely amongst US policymakers, healthcare professionals, parents, teachers, and school administrators. Writers in the group also agreed to try to alert the public to the issue by submitting articles and editorials to a variety of publications.

The February meeting was sponsored by the Center for the Spiritual Foundations of Education at Teachers College, Columbia University, under a grant from the Fetzer Institut, and by Sunbridge College. Joan Almon also helped to organize and moderate the meetings which marked the birth of the Alliance.

'Alone there isn't much we can do', she told the group; 'But if we stand together, there's an immense amount that we can do'.

For further information and a list of national contacts:

Brazil
Alianca para Infancia
Luiza Lameirao e Ute Craemer, Av. Tomas de Souza 552
05836-350 Sao Paulo
Tel: (+55) 11 585 15370 Fax: (+55) 11 585 11089
Email: ascmazul@amcham.co.br
Website: www.sab.org.br/monteazul

Germany
The Alliance for Childhood, c/o International Waldorf Kindergarten Association, D-70188 Stuttgart, Heubergstrasse 18, Germany E-mail:- Inter.waldorf@t-online.de

Sweden
Alliance for Childhood
Dragonvagen 13, S-177675 Jarfalla
Tel/Fax: (+46) 85835 8516
E-mail: sekretariatet@waldorf.se

United Kingdom
The Alliance for Childhood, Kidbrooke Park, Forest Row, East
Sussex, RH18 5JA, UK   E-mail:- alliance@waldorf.compulink.co.uk

United States of America
The Alliance for Childhood, PO Box 444, College Park, MD
20741, USA   E-mail:- jalmon@erols.com

APPENDIX 4

Contacts and Resources

Useful Contacts – International

Steiner Waldorf Early Childhood Education

There are over 40 Steiner Waldorf Kindergartens in Britain (for children aged 3 to 6 years of age), together with Parent and Toddler Groups and playgroups. There are Kindergartens in many countries – see contacts below, or contact the International Waldorf Kindergarten Association in Germany for more information.

Australia
Contact: Dr Renate Long-Breipohl
44 Manor Road, Hornsby NSW 2077
Tel: (+61) 02 9476 6222 Fax: (+61) 02 9940 3039
E-mail: breipohl@smartchat.net.au

Germany
International Waldorf Kindergarten Association
D-70188 Stuttgart, Heubergstrasse 18, Germany
Tel: (+49) 711 925 740 Fax: (+49) 711 925 747
E-mail: Inter.Waldorf@t-online.de

New Zealand
Contact: Marjorie Theyer
c/o Kindergarten Training Course, Taruna College,
Havelock North, Hawkes Bay, 33 Te Matu Peak Road
Tel: (+64) 06 8777 174 Fax: (+64) 06 8777 014

South Africa
Contact: Peter van Alphen
c/o Centre for Creative Education
PO Box 280, Plumstead 7801
Tel: (+27) 21 7976 802 Fax: (+27) 21 7977 095

United Kingdom
Steiner Waldorf Schools Fellowship
Kidbrooke Park, Forest Row, East Sussex
RH18 5JA, United Kingdom
Tel: (+44) 01342 822115 Fax: (+44) 01342 826004
E-mail: mail@waldorf.compulink.co.uk
Website: www.compulink.co.uk/~waldorf

USA and Canada
Waldorf Early Years Childhood Association of North America
285 Hungry Hollow Road, Spring Valley, NY 10977
Tel: (+1) 914 352 1690 Fax: (+1) 914 352 1695

Useful Contacts – United Kingdom

Early Education
(The British Association for Early Childhood Education)
136 Cavell Street, London, E1 2JA
Human Scale Education

96 Carlingcott, Bath BA2 8AW
Tel: (+44) 01275 332516

Let The Children Play

An organisation of parents campaigning for play-based education for young children.

Let The Children Play
Hillview, Portway Hill, Lamyatt, Shepton Mallet
Somerset, BA4 6NJ, United Kingdom
Tel: (+44) 01749 813260 or 01749 813971
E-mail: info@letthechildrenplay.org.uk
Website: www.letthechildrenplay.org.uk

Montessori Society

The Montessori approach to child education is based on the belief 'that every child has creative potential, the drive to learn and the right to be treated as an individual'. Contact address below for more information and details of Maria Montessori training courses.

Montessori Society AMI UK
26 Lyndhurst Garden, London NW3 5NW
Tel: (+44) 020 7435 7874 Fax: (+44) 020 7431 8096

Parentline Plus

Offers support, advice and information to anyone parenting a child. Runs Parent Network courses and a freephone helpline.

Parentline Plus
520 Highgate Studios, 53-59 Highgate Road, Kentish Town
London NW5 1TL, United Kingdom
Tel: (+44) 020 7204 5500 Fax: (+44) 020 7284 5501
E-mail: centraloffice@parentlineplus.org.uk
Website: www.parentlineplus.org.uk
Helpline: 0808 800 2222

Rainbow Trust Children's Charity

Provides family-centred care for children with life-threatening or terminal illness, and their families, at times of crisis.

Rainbow Trust
Claire House, Bridge Street, Leatherhead
Surrey KT22 8BZ
Tel: 01372 363438 Fax: 01372 363101
E-mail: enquiries@rainbowtrust.org.uk
Website: www.rainbowtrust.org.uk

Winston's Wish

A grief support programme for bereaved children and their families. Can provide a list of useful resources, annotated reading lists and information on training.
Winston's Wish
Gloucestershire Royal Hospital, Great Western Road
Gloucester, GL1 3NN
Tel: 01452 394377 Fax: 01452 395656
E-mail: info@winstonswish.org.uk
Website: www.winstonswish.org.uk

A Note on Rudolf Steiner

Rudolf Steiner was born on the borders of Austria and Hungary in 1861. From his early childhood years he experienced that behind all natural phenomena there existed a world of active thought forms which gave them their unique characteristics. Like William Wordsworth before him, all nature was suffused by a celestial light. Steiner's insight grew in clarity and blossomed into a rich source of investigation, leading in turn to many practical applications. New initiatives have been developed in the most varied fields, such as:

- Camphill villages for children and adults with special needs;
- a holistic approach to medicine, extending the art and science of healing;
- a natural-medicine pharmaceutical company, Weleda;
- Steiner Waldorf education;
- a self-sustaining organic agricultural system known as the biodynamic method;
- new forms of architecture and painting;
- an ethical banking system, e.g. TRIODOS.

Further information can be obtained from:

Rudolf Steiner House
35 Park Road, London, NW1 6XT
Tel: 020 772 3400 Fax: 020 772 44364
E-mail: rsh@cix.compulink.co.uk

World List of Rudolf Steiner Waldorf School Associations

The full list of kindergartens, schools and training courses, together with information for countries not listed below (running to some 80 pages in all), can be obtained from the Pedagogical Section of the School of Spiritual Science, Goetheanum, CH-4143 Dornach, Switzerland. *Full title*: '*World List of Rudolf Steiner (Waldorf) Schools and Teacher Training Centers, Stand Februar 2000*', Herausgegeben vom Bund der Freien Waldorfschulen e.V., Heidehofstrasse 32, D-70184, Stuttgart (*Tel.* ++49 (0)711-21042-0; *e-mail* bund@waldorfschule.de)

With thanks to the publisher for permission to reproduce this (abbreviated) list; and to the editor of the journal *Steiner Education*, Dr Brien Masters, for permission to use that journal's list summary.

AUSTRALIA: Association of Rudolf Steiner Schools in Australia, 213 Wonga Road, Warranwood, Victoria, Australia, 3134

AUSTRIA: Österreichische Vereinigung freier Bildungsstätten auf anthroposophischer Grundlage, Endresstrasse 100, A-1230 Wien

BELGIUM: Federatie van Rudolf Steinerscholen in Vlaanderen, Kasteellaan 54, B-9000 Gent

CANADA: Association of Waldorf Schools of North America, c/o David Alsop, 3911 Bannister Road, Fair Oaks, CA 95628, USA;

Ontario: Waldorf School Association of Ontario, 9100 Bathurst Street, Thornhill, Ontario L4J 8CF, Canada

DENMARK: Sammenslatningen af Rudolf Steiner Skoler i Denmark, Strandvejen 102, DK-8000 Århus

ESTONIA: Eesti Waldorfkoolide Ühendus, 14 Koidula Tänav, EE2100, Rakvere, Estonia

FINLAND: Steinerpedagogiikan seura ry-Föreningen- för Steinerpedagogik rf, c/o Lea Blafield, Jyväskylän Rudolf-Steiner-koulu, Honka harjuntie 6, FIN 40600 Jyväskylä

FRANCE: Fédération des Ecoles Rudolf Steiner en France, 11 rue de Villaines, F-091370 Verrieres-le-Buisson

GERMANY: Bund der Freien Waldorfschulen e.V., D-70184 Stuttgart, Heidehofstrasse 32

IRELAND: Irish Steiner Waldorf Education Association, Raheen Road, Tuamgraney, County Clare

ITALY: Associazone Amici Scuola, via Clerici 12, 1-22030 Camnage Volta (COMO)
LATVIA: Lettishe Assoziation für Waldorf-pädagogik, Pirma iela 26a, Rigarajons, LV 2164

LUXEMBOURG: Veräin fir Waldorfpädagogik Lëtzebuerg, 45 Rue de l'Avenir, L 1147 Luxembourg

NETHERLANDS: Bond van Vrije Scholen, Hoofdstraat 14 B, NL-3972 LA Driebergen
NEW ZEALAND: Federation of Rudolf Steiner Schools, PO Box 888, Hastings, Hawke's Bay

NORWAY: Steinerskolene i Norge, Prof. Dahlsgt. 30, N-0260 Oslo

ROMANIA: Federatia Waldorf din Romania, Bd.Marasti nr.59, sector 1, RO-71331 Bucuresti

SLOVENIA: Drustvo prijateljev, waldorfike sole, Rodiceva 2,61000 Ljubljana, Slovenia

SOUTH AFRICA: Southern African Federation of Waldorf Schools, PO Box 67587, Bryanston, Transvaal, 2021 Johannesburg
SWEDEN: Waldorfskolefederationen, Fridhemsgata 17, S-12240 Stockholm

SWITZERLAND: Koordinationsstelle der Rudolf Steiner Schulen in der Schweiz, Robert Thomas, Carmenstrasse 49, CH-8032 Zürich

UNITED KINGDOM: Steiner Waldorf Schools Fellowship, Kidbrooke Park, Forest Row, East Sussex RH18 5JA

USA: Association of Waldorf Schools of North America, Chairman, 3911 Bannister Road, Fair Oaks, CA 95628

List of Further Reading

This book is intended, as the title suggests, to be an introduction to Steiner Waldorf early childhood education. The theme of each individual chapter could justify a book in itself; indeed, many colleagues from around the world have shared their experience and insight in various publications. The following books will deepen the reader's understanding of the aims and practice introduced in *Free to Learn*, and facilitate the exploration of a particular theme in greater depth.

The contact list (below) provides a contact for finding out names and addresses of the main publishers of Anthroposophical and Steiner Waldorf literature.

Books by Rudolf Steiner

The Child's Changing Consciousness, Anthroposophic Press, Hudson, New York, 1996

The Education of the Child and Early Lectures on Education, Anthroposophic Press, Hudson, New York, 1996

Human Values in Education, Rudolf Steiner Press, London, 1971

The Renewal of Education, Steiner Schools Fellowship Publications, Forest Row, 1981

The Roots of Education, Rudolf Steiner Press, London, 1968

Rudolf Steiner: An Autobiography, Steinerbooks, Blauvelt, New York, 1980

The Study of Man, Anthroposophic Press, London, 1947; republished as *The Foundations of Human Experience*, Anthroposophic Press, Hudson, New York, 1996

The Threefold Social Order, Anthroposophic Press, Hudson, New York, 1972

Towards Social Renewal, London, 1977

Works by Other Authors

Aeppli, Willi, *The Care and Development of the Senses*, Steiner Schools Fellowship Publications, Forest Row, 1993

Aeppli, Willi, *Rudolf Steiner Education and the Developing Child*, Anthroposophic Press, Hudson, New York, 1986

Alliance for Childhood, *Fool's Gold: A Critical Look at Computers in Childhood*, College Park, MD, 2000

Baldwin, Rahima, *You Are Your Child's First Teacher*, revised edn, Celestial Arts, Berkeley, 2000 (orig. 1989)

Britz-Crecelius, Heidi, *Children at Play: Preparation for Life*, Inner Traditions International, New York, 1986

Carey, Diana and Large, Judy, *Festivals, Family and Food*, Hawthorn Press, Stroud, 1982

Carlgren, Frans, *Education towards Freedom: Rudolf Steiner Education: A Survey of the Work of Waldorf Schools throughout the World*, Lanthorn Press, East Grinstead, 1993

Childs, Gilbert, *Education and Beyond: Steiner and the Problems of Modern Society*, Floris Books, Edinburgh, 1996

Childs, Gilbert, *Steiner Education in Theory and Practice*, Floris Books, Edinburgh, 1991

Cooper, Stephanie and others, *The Children's Year*, Hawthorn Press, Stroud, 1987

Coplen, Dotty, *Parenting a Path through Childhood*, Floris Books, Edinburgh, 1988

Cuisick, Linda, *Waldorf Parenting Handbook*, St George Publications, New York, 1984

Davy, Gudrun and Voors, Bon, *Lifeways*, Hawthorn Press, Stroud, 1986

Easton, Stewart, *Man and World in the Light of Anthroposophy*, Anthroposophic Press, Hudson, New York, 1975

Elkind, David, *The Hurried Child: Growing up Too Fast Too Soon*, A. A. Knopf, New York, 1987

Elkind, David, *Mis-education: Pre-schoolers at Risk*, A. A. Knopf, New York, 1987

Frommer, Eva, *Voyage through Childhood into the Adult World: A Guide to Child Development*, Hawthorn Press, Stroud, 1969

Glöckler, Michaela and Goebel, Wolfgang, *A Guide to Child Health*, Floris Books, Edinburgh, 1990

Goleman, Daniel, *Emotional Intelligence: Why It Can Matter More than IQ*, Bloomsbury, London, 1996

Grunelius, Elizabeth, *Early Childhood Education and the Waldorf School Plan*, Waldorf School Monographs, New Jersey, 1974

Harwood, A. C., *The Recovery of Man in Childhood*, Anthroposophic Press, Hudson, New York, 1958

von Heydebrand, Caroline, *A Study of the Growing Soul*, Anthroposophical Publishing Co., London, 1946

Jaffke, Freya, *Work and Play in Early Childhood*, Floris Books, Edinburgh, 1996

Jenkinson, Sally, *The Genius of Play*, Hawthorn Press, Stroud, 2001

Konig, Karl, *The First Three Years of the Child*, Anthroposophic Press, Hudson, New York, 1969; *also* Floris Books, Edinburgh, 1998

Large, Martin, *Who's Bringing Them Up? How to Break the TV Habit*, 2nd edn, Hawthorn Press, Stroud, 1992

Lissau, Rudi, *Rudolf Steiner: Life, Work, Inner Path and Social Initiatives*, Hawthorn Press, Stroud, 1987

Meyer, Rudolf, *The Wisdom of Fairy Tales*, Floris Books, Edinburgh, 1987

Meyerkort, Margret and Lissau, Rudi, *The Challenge of the Will Expressions with Young Children*, Rudolf Steiner College Press, USA, 2000

Molt, Emil, *Emil Molt and the Beginnings of the Waldorf School Movement*, Floris Books, Edinburgh, 1991

Patterson, Barbara and Bradley, Pamela, *Beyond the Rainbow Bridge: Nurturing Our Children from Birth to Seven*, Michaelmas Press, Amesbury, Mass.

Postman, Neil, *The End of Education*, A. A. Knopf, New York, 1995

Salter, Joan, *The Incarnating Child*, Hawthorn Press, Stroud, 1987

Schwartz, Eugene, *Millennial Child*, Anthroposophic Press, Hudson, New York, 1999

Soesman, Albert, *Our Twelve Senses*, Hawthorn Press, Stroud, 1998

Strauss, Michaela, *Understanding Children's Drawings*, Rudolf Steiner Press, London, 1978

Thompson, John, Oldfield, Lynne and others, *Natural Childhood*, Gaia Books, London, 1994

Winn, Marie, *The Plug-in Drug: Television, Children, and the Family*, Viking Press, New York, 1985

Getting in touch with Hawthorn Press

What are your pressing questions about the early years?
The Hawthorn Early Years series arises from parents' and educators' pressing questions and concerns – so please contact us with *your* questions. These will help spark new books, workshops or festivals if there is sufficient interest. We will be delighted to hear your views on our Early Years books, how they can be improved, and what your needs are.

Visit our website for details of the Early Years Series and forthcoming books and events:

http://www.hawthornpress.com

Ordering books

If you have difficulties ordering Hawthorn Press books from a bookshop, you can order direct from:

United Kingdom
Scottish Book Source Distribution,
137 Dundee Street, Edinburgh,
EH11 1BG
Tel: 0131 229 6800 Fax: 0131 229 9070

North America
Anthroposophic Press c/o Books International,
PO Box 960,
Herndon, VA 201 72-0960.
Toll free order line: 800-856-8664
Toll free fax line: 800-277-9747

Dear Reader

If you wish to follow up your reading of this book, please tick the boxes below as appropriate, fill in your name and address and return to Hawthorn Press:

 Please send me a catalogue of other Hawthorn Press books.

☐ Please send me details of Early Years events and courses.

Questions I have about the Early Years are:

_____

_____

_____

_____

Name _____

Address _____

_____

_____

Postcode _____ Tel. no. _____

Please return to: Hawthorn Press, Hawthorn House, 1 Lansdown Lane, Stroud, Glos. GL5 1BJ, UK or Fax (01453) 751138